D0343663

WITHDRAWN FROM
THE LIBRARY
UNIVERSITY OF
WINCHESTER

KA 0016251 5

Team Teaching

Team
Teaching

David Warwick

University of London Press Ltd

KING ALFRED'S COLLEGE
WINCHESTER

BASINGSTOKE

371.35
WAR   2197

ISBN 0 340 11788 5 Boards
ISBN 0 340 11789 3 Unibook

Second impression 1971
Copyright © 1971 David Warwick
All rights reserved. No part of this publication may be reproduced or
transmitted in any form or by any means, electronic or mechanical,
including photocopy, recording, or any information storage and retrieval
system, without permission in writing from the publisher.

University of London Press Ltd
St Paul's House, Warwick Lane, London EC4P 4AH
Printed and bound in Great Britain by
Hazell Watson & Viney Ltd, Aylesbury, Bucks

Contents

1   Theoretical basis   9

2   Why team teach?   23

3   Initial planning and preparation   33

4   Patterns of team-work   49

5   Programming the work   60

6   Grouping the children   70

7   Materials and equipment   83

8   The flexible school   95

9   Assessing the work   103

10   Developmental team teaching   113

School plans   opposite 120

Index   121

Acknowledgements

The publishers and author would like to express thanks to the following for all the assistance given in the preparation of this book: Mr A. Aveling, Headmaster of William Robertson School, Welbourn, Lincoln for permission to include the plan on page 101; Messrs Caudill, Rowlett and Scott for permission to include the plan of the domed elementary school reproduced at the back of the book; Mr W. F. Clarke, Headmaster of St Helier Boys School, St Saviour, Jersey, for permission to include the diagram on page 47; the Controller of Her Majesty's Stationery Office for permission to reproduce the plan on page 98; the Education Department, City and County of Bristol and Albert H. Clarke, F.R.I.B.A., A.M.T.P.I., City Architect for Bristol for permission to include the extract from the plans of Merrywood Comprehensive School for Boys, Bristol; K. C. Evans, A.R.I.B.A., for permission to reproduce the plans of Wetherby Deighton Gates Junior Middle School and the extract from the plans of Hatfield Middle School, West Riding; Messrs Kitson and Partners, Leeds and E. W. Stanley, B.A., A.R.I.B.A., Dip.T.P., for permission to reproduce the extract from the plans of the John Smeaton Comprehensive School, Leeds; Penguin Books Ltd for permission to reproduce the extract from *The School That I'd Like* edited by E. Blishen; Mrs C. Redfearn, Senior Mistress at Brockington High School, Enderby, Leicestershire for permission to reproduce the extracts on pages 86/87 and 89/90.

Part of chapter 6 first appeared as an article by the author in *New University* (March 1969) and the essence of chapter 10 first appeared as an article by the author entitled 'Introducing Team Teaching' in *Ideas* (October 1969).

To – Tony, Neil, Fred, Brian, Colin,
John Bl., John Bk., John Gm., David,
Ralph, Pat, Stuart, Jenny, Derek,
Grace and Hazel—*the Henbury team, 1963–67.*

'This is a school! A place where
people together learn to live
together and love one another, where
people learn to reason, learn to
understand and above all learn to
think for themselves. School was not
invented just for little people to
become the same as the big people,
but for the pupils to learn how to
live and let live. Money is not what
is needed so much as common sense,
and the school I would like – in fact,
the school I long for – would be a
thing of the present. Now!'

Judith, 13

(from *The School That I'd Like*, edited
by Edward Blishen, Penguin, 1969)

1. *Theoretical basis*

> 'I am tired of hearing that the hope of
> my country lies in my generation. If
> you give me the same indoctrination as
> a child, how can you expect me to be
> any different from you?'
>
> *Fifteen-year-old girl*[1]

Team teaching has been described in many different ways. Much has been written about it in terms of classroom organization, teacher deployment, and curricular innovation, but far less is heard about ultimate aims, the *raison d'être* behind the whole process.

This may be because such principles are regarded as self-evident within the administrative complexities and hierarchical structures of some such schemes. More probably a reluctance to justify team teaching on educational rather than organizational grounds stems from a belief that no such theoretical basis exists and that, because of this, it cannot be recognized as a technique in its own right at all.

Two very different concepts are here at issue and are embodied in two distinct schools of thought. To some teachers and educationalists team teaching is exactly what its name implies – an economic and fairly democratic way of organizing a school. In this case it offers a convenient administrative framework within which existing structures can survive with slight, if any, modification. To others, though, team teaching represents far more. It can be seen as no less than a return to first principles; a re-orientation of the curriculum so that the needs of both teacher and taught are more fully met. As such team teaching has a theoretical basis of

---

[1] Quoted Blishen, E. (ed.), *The School That I'd Like* (Penguin, 1969), p. 7. Quotations at the beginning of each chapter are taken from this source.

its own, and this basis is in strong contrast to existing modes of secondary school organization.

Pyramids of power

The nature and structure of authority within the contemporary secondary school can be thought of in terms of a pyramid. At the apex there is the headmaster, immediately below him is his senior administrative staff, whilst the rest of the structure is composed of blocks which we call subject departments. These blocks are themselves pyramidal in design, having their own 'heads', their 'posts of special responsibility', and their 'assistant teachers'. Further emphasis is given to the hierarchical nature of the whole by the fact that, although they are similar in shape, these departmental divisions vary in size according to the relative importance assigned to each by the headmaster.

At the very base of the pyramid are usually found the one-teacher departments – Religious Education, Technical Drawing, Domestic Science, Music, etc., and those valuable fragments – the 'general subject' teachers. Rather like the outlaws of the Middle Ages, these men and women tend to lack the security of belonging to a recognized sub-group – in this case a 'department' – through which their views can be channelled and in which they can find full expression.

The model, of course, is an idealized one and will vary in particular from school to school. Church schools, for example, will attach far greater importance to religious education than is probable elsewhere; schools with good sporting records may well wish to maintain athletic standards by greater emphasis upon P.E. and games. With this reservation in mind, the model described above can be represented diagramatically (see opposite).

This pattern has had a profound effect upon the nature of what is taught and the methods employed in getting such material across. It has given a fragmentary character to the curriculum by dividing it into segments, allocating specific teachers to these divisions and, presumably on the assumption that it is their task to disgorge such pre-digested information, has arranged the whole school into divisions of about thirty to forty, which are called 'classes' or 'forms'. This complement is taken as being the maximum with which one teacher can possibly cope.

Certain assumptions are inherent in this whole concept. A

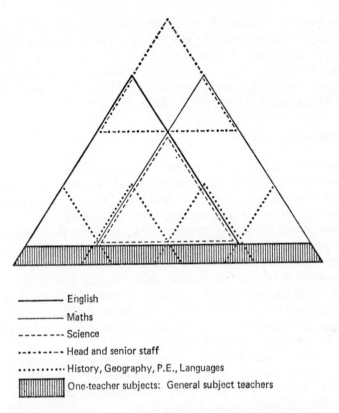

——————— English
——————— Maths
– – – – – – – Science
•••••••••••• Head and senior staff
••••••••••••• History, Geography, P.E., Languages
▓▓▓▓▓ One-teacher subjects: General subject teachers

Secondary school organization – the conventional model

uniform size of group pre-disposes a uniform kind of approach; groups of thirty to forty children and a division into academic subjects invites an approach which is teacher-centred in method, subject-orientated in design, and separatist in approach. Power over curriculum planning and implementation is concentrated almost exclusively into the hands of the headmaster, and it becomes possible for the worth of a teacher to be considered solely in terms of what he has to offer within the confines of a single department. Very real and very valid contributions to be made by smaller departments, or by individuals within those departments, may be structured out of the system, whilst the very nature of the design itself ensures that there will always be more individuals at the base than at the top of the pyramid, thus increasing the possibility of frustration. But perhaps the most serious of all the effects that the 'pyramid' model has had is the diverting of attention away from the real needs of the children to those of the now isolated subject-disciplines; an almost exclusive concentration upon knowledge, which has come to be regarded in terms of progressive revelation – a concept enshrined in the structure and composition of the countless schools erected in its honour.

Team approaches

Team teaching makes no such assumptions. It takes as its starting-point the needs of the children and attempts to structure them as fully as possible into the work of a school. It recognizes that the size and composition of a group must be directly related to the nature of the work it is to perform. It questions the notion that the requirements of either teacher or pupil are best served by an arbitrary division into subject-departments each working in isolation from the others. It does not assume, as far too many of our syllabuses do, that the only contribution to the classroom situation comes from the man at the front of the room, and searches for new forms of organization in which the individual and the functional group can play a far greater part.

Having questioned the uniformity and composition of conventional groupings, the traditional structure of the time-table is also in doubt. Just as groups will be of different sizes according to the kind of work they are doing – in other words functional rather than organizational units – so the optimum length of time allotted for the task in hand will vary. The forty-minute formal lesson may be admirably suited to a group of thirty-six children all learning together from one teacher, but does it equally serve the needs of a large group of 150? And is it in any way satisfactory for a small group of five or six children actively engaged on a project?

Traditionally our time-tables – the visible expression of the pyramid model described above – have not permitted groupings as diverse as this to exist. Nor has it been possible to vary the length of period in accordance with the nature of the work being done. We have tended to be preoccupied with notions such as one teacher – one class, the forty-minute period, the requirements of the subject disciplines, and the supremacy of the headmaster as source and fount of all curricular planning. In the past it has not been considered possible that teachers could actually co-operate to allow such ideas to emerge, let alone that they themselves could take responsibility for the design and planning of large areas of the curriculum. The tendency has been to consider the differences that exist between the different elements within the curriculum as a whole rather than concentrating upon similarities or areas where they overlap.

As long as traditional academic structures remain, teachers will feel impelled to work in isolation from one another – in their classroom, in their department, in their preparation. But as soon as they think and act co-operatively changes such as those outlined above become possible. Hence the title 'team teaching'.

The personal element

When teachers are prepared to work together with their own contribution and the needs of the children more fully in mind new organizational patterns begin to emerge. The approach is now far more horizontal in design both from the content and the teacher-relationship point of view. Fresh areas of work may be defined, but more commonly subjects which have remained isolated begin to merge into larger units – the 'Humanities', the 'Aesthetics', the 'Sciences', etc.

The curriculum thus becomes less fragmentary in design, less authoritarian by nature. Those involved in the implementation of the work now have an active part to play in the planning of it and, alongside this, a new spirit is often engendered. Teachers now have far more of a vested interest in the school where they work; greater loyalty towards something they have helped to create and are actively engaged in sustaining.

In short, team teaching re-asserts the importance of people, and their relationships or reactions one to another, within the context of a school. Audio-visual aids, subject-divisions, classroom utilization, time-tabling, size of class, composition of group, academic syllabus – all were initially introduced to assist individual learning. As such they are excellent servants. The real danger becomes apparent when these factors move from the periphery to the centre of the educative process; from a subsidiary to a key position, as they have done in recent years. Team teaching attemps to redress the balance, to ensure that the individual – be he teacher or taught – is not compressed into preconceived moulds. The 'pyramid' model gives way to new structural designs, see page 47, under the influence of team-teaching methods.

American origins

This is the essence of team teaching – a new movement concerned with the quality of education and the re-structuring of our schools so that they promote rather than impede its advance.

It had its origins in the America of the mid-1950s. Drawing strength from an alliance with several of the great universities, and championed by bodies such as the National Association of Secondary School Principals[1] and the National Education Association,[2] by 1964 it had caught the imagination of some 1 500 teachers, whilst about 45 000 pupils were being instructed under team-teaching methods.[3]

The 1959 Report *Images of the Future* suggested that three broad groupings of pupils might replace conventional classes and that each of these groupings could have specific roles to play in the work of a school. Forty per cent of the scheduled time might be spent in large groups of about one hundred, where the emphasis would be on pupil stimulation, motivation, enrichment, planning of activities, etc. Teachers in this area would be specialists and a wide range of audio-visual aids needed. Another forty per cent of the time would be spent by pupils in small groups of twelve to fifteen, the teacher acting as counsellor or consultant. Finally, twenty per cent of the time available would be spent on individual study or in groups of two or three. Here a variety of activities would be involved – reading, research, experimentation, writing, listening to pre-recorded tapes, viewing photographic material, and so on, under the guidance of a tutor.

This flexibility is described by M. W. Barnes:

> 'Team classes allow many techniques. For purposes of dis-
> cussion, the group may be divided into small units. When a
> panel is reporting, all students may be together. For large
> group activities, a room with special equipment may be used.
> In their planning periods, the teachers consider their own

---

[1] See especially their booklets *New Horizons for Secondary School Teachers* (1957) and *Images of the Future* (1959).

[2] See recommendation 25 in the 1963 *Project on the Instructional Program of Public Schools*.

[3] J. T. Shaplin and H. F. Olds (eds.), *Team Teaching* (Harper and Row, 1964), p. 2.

skills and divide the classroom teaching accordingly . . . No teacher is excellent in all phases of the teaching role. One may be good at presenting ideas, while another is best at retrenching the slow learners who missed some of the ideas in the first presentation, or is able to diagnose a learner's needs. Another does well in correcting written expression. Through observing one another and planning together, team teachers deepen their sensitivity of the complexities of teaching and learning.'[1]

Linked with the idea of team teaching, and in some areas a vital part of it, was the concept of 'internships' – students becoming temporary members of a teaching 'team' as part of their professional training. Another aspect was the employment of non-professional 'aides' for duties ranging from the preparation of rooms and materials to the marking of work and classroom supervision. It was hoped that in this way the status, salary, and dignity of the teacher would be improved, resulting in a better entry to the profession both quantitatively and qualitatively.

By 1965 the technique had become extremely sophisticated both in its organization and presentation of material.

'The instructional set-up is not complete without appropriate tools', wrote one of the pioneers, J. Lloyd Trump. 'The large group presentation must include an overhead projector, other projectors, television, recorders, and possibly a flannel board . . . The screen must be reasonably large and tilted properly to minimize the keystone effect . . . Chest microphones and adequate public address systems are other essentials. Independent study workrooms need projection and recording devices that students can operate themselves, books and printed materials, programmed instruction devices, and the specialized tools of the subject.'[2]

Such a battery of equipment may leave the reader stunned. Even so, team-teaching schemes such as this were costed and found to represent no increase in current American spending. The buildings in which they took place were sometimes equally

---

[1]   Barnes, M. W., 'More Time to Teach', in *Atlantic Monthly*, November 1960, p. 130.
[2]   Lloyd Trump, J., 'What is Team Teaching?', in *Education*, February 1965.

elaborate, as can be seen from the plan of the domed school shown at the back of the book.

Ten years after its tentative inception, team teaching was well established. In numerical terms alone one of America's leading educationalists has stated, 'We are at the beginning of one of the greatest changes in classroom organization we have yet experienced in the history of our schools.'[1]

Developments in England

Team teaching reached England in the early 1960s and it was in the schools rather than the universities that it first took root. Developments at primary level favoured such an innovation. Many secondary schools, with a growing tradition of subject-integration, project-method, and group-work, also welcomed such an approach. The movement for the raising of the school-leaving age was gaining momentum, whilst the curriculum offered to most pupils in their final year was coming under heavy critical fire. The value of team teaching in this whole area of the curriculum was soon recognized and to many teachers it became associated with a more outward-looking approach; a desire to link school with the community and future work in a way not previously possible.

Professor K. Lovell's 1965 summary of American team-teaching ventures,[2] and various articles in the educational press, encouraged further implementation on this side of the Atlantic. More schools took up the idea and at first they worked in isolation, without direct contact with one another.

Initial advances, then, were pragmatic, localized, and largely unscientific. From quite an early stage the Americans had been prepared to define team teaching fairly precisely and attempted to confine experimentation within these definitions. The English experience has been quite different. Almost every school to adopt team teaching advanced along lines of its own. Hence the origins of the technique over here are diverse and variegated.

A combination of factors brought this isolation to a close in the mid-1960s. With the formation of the Schools Council in 1964 came a national body charged with the co-ordination and promo-

[1]   Dr R. Anderson, quoted Keith, Blake, and Tiedt, *Contemporary Curriculum in the Elementary School* (Harper and Row, 1968), p. 136.
[2]   Lovell, K. *Team Teaching* (University of Leeds Institute of Education, 1966).

tion of such ventures. Teachers' centres were being established in many parts of the country, whilst a parallel development was an increased interest in curriculum development on the part of the universities and colleges of education. Research projects were set up and trial schemes initiated. Currently the Schools Council have several major investigations in hand, the outcome of which could have a great effect upon team teaching.[1] Advances in the preparation of teaching materials and methods are also being sponsored by the Nuffield Foundation.[2]

In 1967 Mr John Freeman carried out a nation-wide survey of team-teaching developments in this country although, as he states in his Introduction, by its nature this is not a comprehensive account.[3]

He found team teaching was introduced largely to meet a need – staffing problems had to be solved, facilities were inadequate, a framework was needed for mixed-ability groupings, the school-leaving age was to be raised, etc. – and not through its own educational merits. The full potential of team teaching had not been grasped and Mr Freeman cites as evidence of this a failure to relate the size of the group to the nature of the work it is to perform, the overshadowing of small group activities by large

---

[1]   At the time of writing, the following research projects are included in the work of the Council:

A co-operative study of the secondary school curricula in preparation for the raising of the school leaving age, under Dr W. G. A. Rudd at Manchester University School of Education. One of the panels, under the chairmanship of Mr J. J. Close (Headmaster, Harper Green County Secondary School, near Bolton) is investigating team-teaching projects in some forty schools in Lancashire.

Dr R. King, of Exeter University Institute of Education, is heading a study of internal factors in school organization and discipline, whilst Miss E. Richardson is conducting similar research in Bristol comprehensive schools.

Two projects – under Mr L. Stenhouse at Philippa Fawcett College, London, and D. W. Bolam at Keele University Institute of Education – are concerned mainly with the production, testing, and use of teaching materials.

The Schools Council General Studies Project is centred at York University and is also primarily concerned with the 'banking' of materials.

[2]   The Nuffield Foundation is sponsoring the *Humanities Curriculum Project* at Philippa Fawcett College jointly with the Schools Council. The *Resources for Learning Project* of the Nuffield Foundation, under the direction of Mr L. C. Taylor, aims at the provision of materials for group work with third-year children.

[3]   J. Freeman, *Team Teaching in Britain* (Ward Lock, 1969).

'key' presentations, and the slowness with which materials and
equipment are coming to be used in ways dictated by individual
schemes themselves. His book, with its accounts of many schemes currently in operation, serves as an excellent record of progress to date.

Team teaching – a definition

So far no attempt has been made to define exactly what is meant
by the expression 'team teaching' in practical terms. What has
been established, though, is the impossibility of definition other
than in the most general sort of way. A glance at much of the
literature connected with this subject will also confirm the need
to use language that can be readily assimilated by the teacher in
the classroom. Faced with a demand to define team teaching,
there is a tendency to escalate into jargon, the effect of which is
frequently to encapsulate the concept against any form of emula-
tion. Perhaps this is the purpose? Surely, though, any educational
definition should be descriptive rather than prescriptive; promo-
tive rather than inhibitive. Team teaching does not form an
exception to this rule! A short definition might be as follows:

> 'A form of organization in which individual teachers decide
> to pool resources, interests, and expertise in order to devise
> and implement a scheme of work suitable to the needs of
> their pupils and the facilities of their school.'

Certain aspects of this definition need stressing. Team
teaching is *a* form of organization. As such it is one among several
and should not be regarded as the only approach possible.

Next, teachers *decide* to take action. Team teaching is not
imposed upon them from above, nor is it likely to succeed if this
happens. A headmaster may suggest the possibilities of team-work
within his school. He may send selected members of his staff off
on a course to learn more about it, or commission memoranda
upon the subject. Some in-service training may take place. But
unless the staff concerned are enthusiastic about the project, fully
understand it, and are thus prepared to give the time and energy
to make it work, team teaching will be doomed to failure.

Thirdly, team teaching involves a *pooling of resources*. These
'resources' include factors such as specializations, interests,
knowledge, skills, experience, and personality. They also include
more tangible factors such as periods on the time-table, depart-

mental equipment and facilities, free time for meetings, in some cases subject identity, and so on. The success of any team-teaching venture can usually be measured in the amount individual members of the group are prepared to put into it. It runs on the principle that the combined resources of all working in harmony are far greater than the total of each individual component.

Some teams work very well with no acknowledged leader. Meetings have to be chaired, but this responsibility is taken in turns by members of the group. It may be that there is a 'general co-ordinator', a 'team leader', or even a 'head of department'. The essence of team-work, though, lies in the contribution of each individual towards the work as a whole and the co-operation that exists within the team which allows this to emerge. Team teaching is thus precluded if a syllabus is drawn up by the 'leader' without adequate consultation with all concerned, or if portions of a syllabus are allocated to members of the group regardless of their individual capabilities or reactions to it. The title 'co-ordinator' is more descriptive than 'team leader'. The chief function here is surely that of welding the various skills and interests of the group into a unified and workable whole; the emphasis must truly be on an active 'pooling of resources'.

Next, it almost goes without saying that the work must be related to the *facilities of the school*. These include the existing buildings, the equipment possessed, materials available, curricular tradition, personalities concerned, and so on.

Finally, team teaching must centre on the *needs of the pupils*. As has been stated, it is a process whereby staffing and facilities are reconsidered and deployed with this object more directly in mind. It follows that team teaching must be both well-prepared and carefully structured. Initial preparation has to begin several weeks or months before the actual introduction of the scheme, the more obvious general needs of the pupils being built in from the start and individual requirements met by careful grouping and allocation of material. Interests and enthusiasms, captured by an initial stimulus ('lead lesson') and maintained with activity-centred follow-up work, are also built into the project. Such response, or lack of it, will be fed back into the system via team meetings, and so affect future planning.

Other factors which influence choice and arrangement of material as well as the grouping of the children stem less directly, but no less certainly, from their needs. There are the different

requirements at each stage of a child's development; social needs
that can only be met by working alongside others in different kinds
of ways; and the very general requirements needed by youngsters
before they can take their place in society. Educational objectives,
beyond the appreciation of any but the most mature pupil, yet
affecting him keenly, also have to be taken into consideration.
These include concepts such as the fullest possible development of
innate potential, the value of social education both as an aid to this
and as an end in itself, and the importance of such factors as
moral, spiritual, and emotional values.

Team teaching allows concepts such as these to be structured
more directly into the curriculum. Indeed, it is one of the merits of
the technique that it demands a return to first principles; a
challenge to long-cherished aims and objectives. It is a process
which involves – among other factors – matching size and composition of the group to the task in hand; a far more flexible
organization as far as time-tabling and lesson periods are concerned; resulting from this, new utilization of audio-visual material,
equipment, and teaching spaces (the word 'classroom' in many
cases becomes inappropriate); and radical re-thinking of pupil
assessment. For far too long the unique contribution of each
individual has been subordinated to that of the 'class' or 'form';
the needs of the pupils in general to our concept of what they
should know, when they should know it, where it should be given,
and what form it should take. Team teaching at last gives us, or
can give us, a solution to such dilemmas. And this brings us, full
circle, back to the 'essence of team teaching'.

Theoretical basis

The theoretical basis of team teaching can now be seen to depend
upon three separate yet closely interrelated sets of factors. These
are presented diagramatically here.

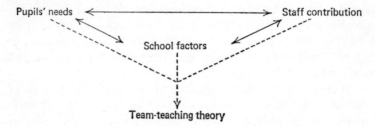

The way forward

Viewed as an educational objective in its own right team teaching can be seen to require far-reaching changes in the way we organize our schools. Well-established academic structures which have served us well in the past become retrogressive elements under a new, more democratic, regime.

It is unlikely, though, that schools will be willing to dismantle long-cherished forms of organization and methods of procedure on hearsay alone. They will, quite rightly, demand team teaching to prove itself in action before such drastic steps are taken. Unfortunately, team teaching cannot do this unless much of the existing framework of a school is abandoned. This accounts for the formalism and rigidity of so many current schemes – the attempt has been made to fit team-teaching techniques into a conventional framework of classes, departments, and techniques. As John Freeman's research (see page 17) clearly shows – it is the organizational aspects of team teaching, quite divorced from its educational implications, that have so far prevailed. And so deadlock is reached. Reformation cannot take place unless fundamental changes are made; yet fundamental changes will not be made unless reformers prove their point in a very practical way!

This situation must be fully accepted and, if progress is to be made, it must begin from within the existing system. It is, perhaps, an essential part of educational reform that each stage in the process must be experienced by those responsible for its implementation. Revision cannot take place unless it begins from the security of a known situation and unless, at each step forward, the confidence of those concerned is won.

Much of what follows, then, deals with the mechanics of establishing team teaching in the everyday school situation; of allowing practising teachers to gain progressive insights into teamwork and assisting them to evolve new forms of organization suited to each stage of the process. The developmental aspect of team teaching is, after all, one of its most characteristic features.

Further reading

American concepts of team teaching and its development in the United States are fully described in *Team Teaching* by J. T. Shaplin and H. F. Old (Harper and Row, 1964), and there is also

a good account in *Team Teaching, Bold New Venture*, edited by
D. W. Beggs III (Indiana University Press, 1964). Brief sum-
maries of the key features from the American point of view appear
in *The Revolution in the Schools* (pp. 93–100), edited by R. Cross
and J. Murphy (Harbinger, Brace and World, 1964), and *The
Changing Secondary School Curriculum*, edited by W. M. Alexan-
der (Holt, Rinehart and Winston, 1967), see the article by J.
Lloyd Trump on pages 258–264.

K. Lovell's booklet *Team Teaching* (University of Leeds
Institute of Education, 1967) attempts to relate American developments in this field to the English situation, and Charity James has
some very salient points to make in her book *Young Lives at Stake*
(Collins, 1968, see especially pp. 57–59). *Team Teaching in Britain*
by J. Freeman (Ward Lock, 1969) is the only comprehensive
survey of team-teaching schemes being developed in this country.

The early work of the Schools Council is summarized in two
of its own publications – *Challenge and Response, the First Year's
Work* (HMSO, 1965) and *The First Three Years, 1964–7* (HMSO,
1968). There is also an interesting symposium of extracts from
previous publications – *The New Curriculum* (HMSO, 1967).
General surveys of work in progress are also to be found in
Modern Curriculum Developments in Britain (CREDO, 1968) and
J. Carmichael's *Educational Revolution* (Longmans, 1968).

Contemporary developments in curricular planning, theory,
and practice are probably best followed in the various journals
dealing with such matters. Important here are – *The Journal of
Curriculum Studies* (Editors P. H. Taylor, S. Morris, and J. F.
Kerr; bi-annually, Collins); *Dialogue* (Schools Council newsletter;
three a year; Curwen Press); *Ideas* (journal of the Goldsmiths
College Curriculum Laboratory; editor, L. Smith); *General
Studies Project Newsletter* (University of York; editor, R. Lord);
and the HMSO Curriculum Bulletins. There is also a very worthwhile series of pamphlets issued from time to time by the Univer-
sity of Exeter Institute of Education under the general title
Themes in Education.

2. *Why team teach?*

'They say that Rome has not died, she
only sleeps –
Yet through all my pages of Latin
verbs
I have not felt her stir.'

Gillian, 15

The origins, development, and definition of team teaching in theoretical terms will not be sufficient for our purpose. Before it is introduced at any level, further information of a practical kind will be required by those who are to take part in it. A lot of time, energy, and enthusiasm will have to be expended in order to initiate such a scheme and keep it going. What exactly can be hoped for in return? Is team teaching really a viable proposition for a headmaster or head of department? What are its characteristic features?

Economic factors

It seems that the emphasis now is upon large secondary schools and this means subject departments of three, four, or even five members. The traditional way of organizing such a department is for its head, in view of his teaching experience and academic qualifications, to produce a syllabus which is then taught by him and members of his department throughout the school. The same material is usually given to all the classes in the same year. Thus, in history, all Year One may be studying Prehistoric Man, all Year Two the Anglo-Saxons and Romans, and all Year Three the Middle Ages. In a six-form-entry school this means that the same lesson will be given six times. It means that, if audio-visual material is used, it will tend to be used in the most uneconomic fashion. There may, for example, be a filmstrip on 'The Mediaeval Village'. Is this to be used six times with six different groups? If so, this is going to be wasteful of strip, projector, bulbs, electricity, blacked-out rooms (always in short supply) and, above all, that most important factor – teacher-energy.

When this filmstrip is to be used could it not be shown to two large groupings rather than six smaller ones? If so, all these economies would be effected. This is frequently done when films are hired from distributing agencies, and it is not really such a radical step to extend the process to one's own audio-visual equipment. In fact most lessons of a factual nature can as easily be given to large groupings as they can to small ones. Cannot this form of organization, then, be further extended within large departments? A lesson given twice to 120 children on each occasion can be as effective as the same one given six times to 36 children. Actually, it will probably be more effective, as a good deal more thought and preparation is likely to be given to it, and there is less chance of the teacher concerned relying solely upon 'chalk and talk'. He will probably break up his exposition with slides, tape-recorded material, film, or filmstrip. Also there is not so much chance that the approach will have become 'stale' through over-exposure. Opportunities there will have to be for questions, recapitulation, and individual approaches to the subject matter, and here smaller groupings are obviously more suitable. Further periods will therefore have to be set aside for following up large sessions under the direction of the class teacher. Groupings in these follow-up periods may even differ in size. One teacher may agree to supervise a larger number of pupils than usual for work of a fairly formal nature, thus releasing a colleague to lead smaller groups in discussion or helping with project work.

Structuring in enthusiasm

Not all lessons are factual, though. Some attempt is often made to give the 'feel' of a period in history, evoke the physical sensations of a geographical location, awaken sympathy with a character in fiction, or get spiritual concepts across. It may be that a lesson is to be given on 'Society in the Middle Ages', 'Life in the Australian Outback', or 'Jewish reactions to Jesus'. This sort of thing can really only be done by the specialist, the teacher who has devoted a good deal of time and thought to the specific problem, has read widely around it, who has experienced it personally, and whose enthusiasm for it is self-evident.

Under our conventional form of organization such enthusiasm is restricted to the class or classes that the teacher in question takes. All teachers within a department are called upon to teach all – or most – aspects of their subject. An historian may know all there is to know about Georgian England. He teaches this as part of his normal work and it may take up to two or three terms out of a five year course. The rest of his teaching-load will probably be devoted to covering, as part of the syllabus, most other periods of British and European history. As an historian he will find these interesting, but for none of them will he feel the over-riding concern that he does for his own area of specialization. It will be no coincidence that the children he teaches will tend to feel this way also. Enthusiasm is contagious. Moreover, we are all inclined to devote most of our time and energy to those parts of a syllabus we find personally rewarding. And this is just another way of saying that these parts of the syllabus are the best taught.

But why should this teacher's enthusiasm for the Georgian period be restricted to just the classes he teaches? Is there no way of getting this across to a wider range of pupils? In fact, in the same way that the factual lesson might be given in two large sessions with adequate follow-up in smaller groups, can't the individual expertise and experience of members of the department be shared by a total year group? Experience has shown that it is just this type of lesson (the one where feelings, imagination, and disciplined insight are required) that goes extremely well in the charged atmosphere of the 'lead lesson' about which I have been writing.

Deployment of staff

The lead lesson, given to a large group, and follow-up periods for individual classes, are two characteristic features of team teaching as it has developed in this country. By making use of them, economy is effected, staff are used more efficiently, teachers feel a greater sense of 'belonging' to a department, and individual skills are put at the disposal of all the children.

Who is to take these mass sessions? Obviously this will be the teacher with most enthusiasm or knowledge about the topic concerned. If a department has gone this far, it is but a short step to the principle that those most enthusiastic about a particular part of the syllabus should be those most closely involved in it.

From here it does not take a great stretch of the imagination to envisage a syllabus evolved directly out of the individual enthusiasms and expertise of departmental members.

Here a third element in team teaching enters the discussion – the deployment of teachers to areas and methods in which they feel most 'at home'. Their function now becomes a dual one. The channelling of the greater part of their energies into the preparation of effective lead lessons and activity follow-up material for the complete year group. This is limited to those areas in which they have expressed preference or have specialized knowledge. Secondly, they also have a responsibility towards a group or groups of children within the total year-group. They must get to know these children really well so that they can adapt follow-up material prepared by other members of the team to suit their individual needs. In turn, the way these smaller groups have reacted to the work in hand is fed back into the system via the group leader (class teacher).

It should be stressed that no claims are being made that teaching hours will be saved. They will not. What is especially attractive about team teaching, though, is that it uses a teacher's time and energies far more economically and effectively.

Experience-centred work

Team-teaching is also relevant to the secondary school curriculum in another very practical way. Traditionally our schools have held themselves aloof from society at large. A part of the neighbourhood, yet essentially apart from it, they have been regarded both from within and without as oases of culture in a wilderness of ignorance and anarchy.

Today there is a strong movement away from this position. Many teachers are seeking to make their appeal less vicarious, more experience-centred. At the upper end of the school far more realistic links are being formed with the world of work, yet current conventions of school organization do not help. Most subjects have two or three single periods each week. They cannot spare the time for such experimentation and, if they could, forty minutes is totally inadequate. The practice of one man, one class inevitably leads to departments, often even individual teachers, working in complete isolation. Very few people in an average school have a complete picture of the work going on within any one subject or within any one year. When 'class' or 'form' is the unit and an 'agreed syllabus' (whatever the subject!) the basis of instruction, traditional methods are the tools most suited for the task. Traditional methods, though, are based upon the idea of a school within, yet apart from, the community – which is just the concept currently being challenged.

A whole new approach is coming into being. It entails complete afternoons given over to realistic fieldwork of all kindly the availability of two or more members of staff simultaneouss; involved in one project; a breaking away from the conventional form of classroom divisions; and a 'blocking' of the school time-table to give the facilities and space required. It is a process that seeks to cast off the concept of the teacher as the '2-4-7 man' – someone most at home within the two covers of a text-book, the four walls of a classroom, and the seven periods of a school day. In recent years a new phrase – 'the flexible school' – has been coined to cover all these innovations.

Team teaching has an obvious part to play here, just as it has in revising the more conventional subject department. In this case, however, it will be a form of team teaching that cuts across academic boundaries.

Team teaching and integrated studies

The call for closer co-operation between subjects in the secondary school, and for complete integration over certain areas, rests partly on the very practical reasons already given. Behind these, though, are considerations of a more philosophical nature.

Are we to believe, for example, that children experience life in subject divisions? Is a visit to the parish church a rich religious experience, or even *chiefly* a religious experience? And the Tower of London – does this provide food for historical thought only? Come to that, what exactly do we mean when we label various experiences 'historical', 'religious', 'artistic', 'literary', etc.?

The answer will probably be that it is not 'content' that should be considered, but a training in various 'disciplines' or 'skills'. There is a certain way of looking at things which is essentially 'geographical'; there are certain 'historical' skills which must be developed in the course of a child's schooling; there is a separate 'discipline' of religious education which only the specialist can get across, and so on. This one could more easily accept were the specialist teachers more unanimous in their verdict as to what are their respective aims. Ten different historians, for example, are likely to give ten differing opinions as to what their special 'discipline' entails. Yet each will insist that, without it, a pupil's education is incomplete. It also seems to be assumed without question that in team teaching these various skills will be lost rather than strengthened.

At this point I would like to interject a personal, and largely unscientific, note. In the course of my teaching career I have not noticed that excellence or failure in the classroom is confined to certain areas of the curriculum. In other words, teachers do not appear to be good 'science' teachers, using 'good science methods', bad 'English' teachers adopting 'bad English techniques', etc. Rather they tend to be 'good teachers', 'bad teachers', 'indifferent teachers', as the case may be. The methods they adopt seem to be either good, or otherwise, for teaching children – not subjects. Thus a really good teacher appears to succeed in every subject he tackles, and poor teaching will be correspondingly reflected across the complete spectrum of the curriculum.

There may be a separate academic discipline connected with each different subject. Perhaps integration will dilute the excellence of this discipline. Of course, it may be that this whole idea has its roots in the now discarded nineteenth century concept of 'faculty psychology'. Be this as it may, the 'subject skills' here under review appear to take a very subordinate place compared with certain other principles or methods not confined to any one area of the curriculum. The real danger lies in valuing intrinsic academic content more highly than the needs of the individual pupil. Team teaching is unlikely to succumb to this danger. It places the needs of the children above the needs of the subject.

If one accepts the premise that the curriculum of a school can be dissected vertically as well as horizontally, there still remain large areas of overlap. The Crusades – are they to be covered in history lessons or religious education? Can the geography of India be studied without reference to the Hindu faith? When children write an essay on 'The Carbon Cycle', is this an exercise in science or English? Is mime dance or drama? Ancient Egypt – its history, centred firmly upon the annual rise and fall of the Nile and unique location of the country, is geography as well. Its geography is inextricably bound up with its religion. Consider the many gods – those of sky, river, nature, moon, sun, and earth.

The religion of ancient Egypt, though, is also its history. Scientific teaching is needed to explain the reasons behind these once venerated occurrences. Their measurement and presentation brings in mathematics; their depiction has always had a place in the teaching of art.

All these examples, and many more than can be cited here, come from the syllabus of most of our secondary schools.

In all these considerations 'team teaching' and 'integrated studies' are very closely linked. The two phrases are sometimes used as if they were synonymous. This is not exactly so. Any departments wishing to integrate will inevitably find themselves drawn into some form of team organization, however loose or rudimentary this may be. But individual academic departments can practise team teaching along lines such as have already been indicated without any thought or intention of integrating one with another.

Two further areas of gain can be expected from the introduction of team teaching. They lie in the response to this new situation of both members of staff and the children concerned.

Pupil response

Team teaching takes as its starting point the needs of the pupils. A good deal of trouble is gone to in order to reorientate the curriculum with this object more directly in mind. Such reorganization does not go unnoticed, and it is not unusual for a marked change in attitude to be observed. This is especially the case in team-teaching arrangements where special emphasis is placed on an 'open-ended' approach; one where the pupils' reactions to the work in hand decide the direction and scope of the syllabus.

Another area of gain as far as pupils in lower classes are concerned is the easing of the transition from primary to secondary schooling. The large numbers, and hence greater organizational complexity of the secondary school confuse young children. Also the fragmentation of what, to many children, has previously been an 'integrated day' can be most confusing. This whole process within the secondary school has been very well described as

'a series of seven or eight experiences, rigidly differentiated, but basically similar, engineered by the ringing of a bell, upon which nearly everyone moves somewhere else and does something slightly different'.[1]

Team teaching on an interdisciplary basis cuts down the numbers of teachers children have to get to know in their early years of secondary schooling. Normally, this could be as many as ten, each with his own different manner, method, foibles and idiosyncrasies. It reduces the confusion of the 'school day', alluded to above. It also continues the primary school emphasis upon activity-work and discovery methods.

Staff co-operation

Team teaching for the staff represents a break from the isolation of the classroom. Very few teachers can have failed to experience, at some time or another, the gnawing worries – 'Are my methods in line with other peoples?'; 'Am I doing the best I can for my pupils?' For some, this is one of the occupational hazards of the profession. Discussion in the staff-room or at conferences is not really satisfactory in this case; there is always the doubt, all too often well-founded, that ones colleague's 'bark' does not always match up to his classroom 'bite'! Teaching method is also notoriously difficult to describe or assess. The individual teacher is often hard put to say exactly why he employs such an approach, or a certain technique. He knows that it 'works' whilst others have failed, and that is sufficient.

Team-work amongst teachers allows a glimpse, hitherto unlikely to have been afforded, of one's colleagues at work. It gives an opportunity to compare methods and approaches. A far more practical foundation is provided upon which to base discussion and planning. It is also true that, in the course of team teaching, interests and experiences are revealed which hitherto have been unsuspected. Had it not been for this closer co-operation between members of staff, they would have lain dormant and unused within the classroom. Who would have thought that Mr Jones, the R.E. teacher, was an expert in modelling ships? This skill can be put to use in the 'Voyages of Discovery' programme next term. Miss Smith, who is in the Domestic Science Department, actually visited the Lascaux Caves two years ago and has a complete set of

[1]   Rollings, A. B. and Fitton, N.' 'The Henbury File', *New Education,* May 1965, p. 19.

slides. The 'Origins of Religion' is coming up with Year One in two weeks time . . . Did you know that the French master was also fluent in Anglo-Saxon – part of his degree was in Old English – how about bringing him in on 'The Coming of Christianity' with 'The Lord's Prayer' as it was spoken by Alfred the Great?

The point is not that such skills exist. They abound in any school. The tragedy is that, in the average one, neither Mr Jones nor Miss Smith would probably know that the particular lessons were to take place at all and, not being members of the departments concerned, no one would have considered making use of their talents. Here is another aspect of the isolation of the teacher that has been referred to above.

When team teaching cuts across subject barriers, the rewards for teachers are immense. All too often we tend to congregate with others of our own discipline in unilateral conclaves. It can be extremely refreshing, and sometimes salutary, to hear the comments of those trained in other areas of specialization.

Summary

Economy of materials and equipment; a more efficient use of manpower; the structuring into the system of the interests and enthusiasms of individual members of staff; a tailoring of lessons and approach to fit the needs of the pupils; a matching of approach and setting to the type of material concerned; a framework within which subject integration can take place; a good 'bridge' between the closely-knit primary school community and the more impersonal world of the secondary school, a way of involving the classroom teacher more actively and directly with the evolution of a meaningful curriculum – these are some of the by-products of team teaching.

Further reading

There is a good chapter on the possibilities of team teaching in W. K. Richmond's *The Teaching Revolution* (Methuen, 1967, Chapter 3; issued as a paperback in 1969).

More can be learnt about integrating various subjects, and the 'fourfold curriculum' in *Young Lives at Stake* by Charity James (Collins, 1968), 'The Tyranny of Subjects' by A. Hunt (in *Education for Democracy*, Penguin, 1970, pp. 41–9) and Sir Richard

Acland's *A Move to the Integrated Curriculum* (University of Exeter Institute of Education, 1967). A publication called *An Experiment in I.D.E.* is currently expected from this source.

More general reading about such developments within Social Studies is to be found in *Men and Societies*, edited by R. Irvine Smith (Heinemann, 1969) and *The Social Studies in English Education* by V. Rogers (Heinemann, 1969). General reading should also include *Experiments in Education at Sevenoaks* (Constable Young, 1965).

3. Initial planning and preparation

'3D education rather than flat
black-and-white learning.'

Anne, 18

At the very beginning of a team-teaching venture the headmaster's approval will obviously be of vital importance. Before this is sought it is therefore as well to think through the full implications of what is being proposed. Several questions need contemplation by anyone associated with such a scheme.

First, what are the general aims of team teaching? Secondly, are these an improvement upon the objectives currently being sought? If not, are there any specific aims related to the individual school that the technique claims to be able to achieve? Will it, for example, make a more economic and sound use of existing facilities, or will it materially assist the early leavers in their transition from school to work?

In the case of these questions being answered in the affirmative – if the specific or general aims seem valid – consideration will now have to be given to a third point – how radical will the immediate changes be? What will be the cost, both financially, in terms of re-organization, and in possible disruption of routine? An outline plan will be needed at this stage and very careful thought given to all aspects of it. Consideration must be given to the level and area of the curriculum in which the technique is to be introduced; to the necessary pre-requisites in terms of space, manpower and equipment; and to the basic organization of the proposed scheme.

Team teaching with younger children

It must be realized that, just as each level of a secondary school has its own problems and potentialities, team teaching will take on a very different aspect in response. It has a significant role to play in bridging the gap between primary and secondary education. It allows for continuity. The methods and atmosphere of the former are carried over into the more academic framework of the latter; the school day is less artificially broken up and the curriculum not so fragmentary; above all, the children are introduced into their new school as a corporate unit. Rather than being dispersed amongst various isolated classes, much of the work is jointly conducted.

In basic philosophy, team teaching has much in common with the emerging concept of the 'middle school'. It is fortuitous that the technique and an institution so admirably geared for its implementation should have emerged concurrently. Or were both a product of the same wave of educational reform? Whichever view is taken, some form of team organization is likely to become one of the basic structures of such a school, and thus be assured of a lasting place in our educational system.

The characteristics of team teaching at this stage are, as always, related to the needs of the children. They derive from the experience-centred methods which have so transformed the primary school classroom in recent years, emphasis being placed on informality and flexibility. Team teaching will probably not be confined to individual subject departments, even if these exist as such. 'Lead lessons' are unlikely to feature so prominently in the overall pattern, this term being hardly applicable in many instances. They will take place less frequently, be less regular and, when they occur, the stress will be on their value as stimuli for creative thought or in strengthening the basic skills. Schemes will thus take more account of individual or group reaction than is possible in the higher reaches of the secondary school. The environment will feature largely, and one of the bonuses may well be greater parental co-operation.

Team-work in the upper secondary school

These features are also common to many team-teaching ventures operating within the first two years of conventional secondary education, but by the time the third year is reached greater specialization is usually deemed necessary. Future career, individual preference, and examination prospects merit increased consideration. The broad general education – characteristic of the earlier stages – is progressively phased out, its place taken by the series of specialized 'disciplines' that, externally assessed, make up an individual's main qualification when applying for a job. By the time he reaches the sixth form, a pupil can expect to be spending eighty-five per cent of his time on three closely allied subjects.

Schools cannot usually cater for any but a restricted combination of subjects at this level. If you take physics and chemistry, for example, you may well have to drop art and music; if you study art you can easily find yourself sitting for geography as well, although you detest it; an interest in modern languages may preclude all but the most perfunctory treatment of history and religion – two subjects you have previously enjoyed. These options are usually tightly scheduled and clearly defined.

Another common complaint against external examinations is their lack of direct relevance to the contemporary situation. Even in the science subjects their syllabuses seem to have little bearing upon life as it is actually lived. This might be excusable if the examination system achieved what it set out to do – discipline the mind to cope with the problems of living in a complex society. Experience shows this rarely happens. The mind is conditioned to the abstractions of the university syllabus that awaits those who succeed. Students themselves, though, are unanimous in their verdict; the evidence of their performance tacitly concurs – the ingestion of examination teaching is largely unpalatable, its contents soon forgotten. Rather than developing the flexibility required in a rapidly changing society, mental ossification is the constant danger of too early and too narrow a specialization. The 'means' seem to have been sacrificed to the 'ends', but these 'ends' in themselves are out of tune with the age in which we live.

Team teaching has a valuable part to play here. By a voluntary combination of various specialized departments into larger faculties, and a continuation of the basic objectives outlined earlier, too great a specialization at too early an age can be avoided. Flexibility is one of the keynotes of team teaching and this is an important asset in the education of young people who can now expect to learn new skills at least three times in their future career. It is also a means of breaking away from the limited combination of subjects that can be offered at O or A level. A student can now be a member of up to three 'teams' stemming from each of which three or more specialized subjects can be offered for GCE. Given the more flexible arrangements already referred to, his follow-up work can be supervised by tutors covering a wide area of the curriculum. From one confederation of subjects he can be preparing for English, from another for botony, whilst from a third for religious education and ancient history. Throughout this process he is not losing the broad general education into which each separate 'discipline' can be fitted, and he may be grouped in 'tutorials' with other pupils studying a cluster of closely allied subjects. In this way the requirements of practically all fourth and fifth formers can be met. It is the time-table that is being adjusted to fit the pupil, and not vice-versa.

The areas of integration, or association, will vary from school to school depending upon a multiplicity of factors. The usual combinations, however, are:

The Humanities – English, history, geography, religious education.
The Sciences – biology, botony, physics, chemistry, mathematics.
The Aesthetics – music, art.
The Practical Subjects – woodwork, metalwork, craft, needlework, domestic science.

At this stage – from the third year onwards – team teaching will be more formal in nature and increasingly geared to the requirements of a factual syllabus. Emphasis will continue to be placed on creativity, but the assessment of an individual's performance and attitude will be given closer attention. The basic structure of any scheme will probably centre on regular lead lessons and group-centred follow-up work. Large group presentations will now have to be given to smaller numbers as the pupils are larger physically and more adult in their reactions. A hall which holds two hundred first-year children will not take more than two-thirds of this number when they reach the fourth year. Their maturity must also be respected by limiting the numbers somewhat and making lead lessons more adult in content and presentation.

Team teaching and examination classes

Team-work on an interdisciplinary basis may be rejected for one reason or another. This does not preclude a unilateral team approach to examination work. The head of department will almost certainly act as general co-ordinator here, whilst other members of his staff cover various sections or topics within the syllabus. Continuity will be assured by group discussion and general classroom follow-up under the direction of one teacher throughout. Results are generally rewarding from all points of view. The students receive a variety of viewpoints, benefiting from an added depth and range of treatment, made possible by their teachers having longer to prepare their material, and a concentration upon limited areas of research. Each member of the department is also given the opportunity of sharing in examination work while opposing views can also be placed in context in the 'brains trust' type of discussion.

Sixth-form team teaching

At sixth-form level much of the time devoted to 'general' or 'minority' studies could be used more economically and to greater effect by utilizing team-teaching methods. Many schools not in favour of the technique elsewhere do, in fact, deploy groups of their staff for purposes very like those of team teaching during these periods. But why restrict this within individual schools? In the absence of a sixth-form college why not make these students' education as wide and as open as possible?

Certain comprehensive schools in the north of Bristol in 1966 decided to time-table a common general studies afternoon. Each school nominated two teachers who were felt to have something unique to contribute and which should not therefore be restricted to the confines of their own school. They were asked to prepare courses of their choice lasting for two terms. Among these were – 'Great Religions of the World'; 'The Construction of an Astral Telescope'; 'Speaking Russian'; 'Communism, Fascism, and Democracy'. The total sixth-form complement of the schools was then asked to opt for one of these courses, which they then attended for the next sixteen weeks. This kind of organization largely pre-figured the type of approach and treatment they would later be receiving at university or college. It was also team-work carried across the boundaries of school and staffing. One can envisage it extended to examination work also. Team teaching can bridge the gap between school and university, just as it can between primary and secondary education.

The early leaver

In all this the pupil who will not take any external examination – or who traditionally has not been encouraged to – must not be forgotten. It was to meet the needs of this section of our community that team teaching was first established in many schools. The Schools Council have also devoted several of their 'Working Papers' to the curriculum of these pupils.[1]

Schemes need to be very outward-looking. The approach is open-ended and the local environment, both physical and social, is heavily drawn upon. The vocational and practical bias is strong, with some form of careers guidance usually structured into the organization and, in some areas, work experience being practised. The work usually draws upon the resources of a wide range of departments, integration rather than interdisciplinary co-operation normally being required.

The Certificate of Secondary Education is of great importance here. Introduced in 1966 with the needs of these pupils very much in mind, it emphasizes the relevance of each subject to daily life. Its administration and syllabuses are largely the concern of practising teachers, which means that it can be directly geared to the part of the country in which the school is situated. Individual work of a practical nature, such as models, drawings, plans, or photographs, can be accepted as part of the assessment, as can group research projects on topics such as 'The Churches of York', 'The Wildlife of the South Downs', or 'Flight Through the Ages'. If the school opts for a Mode 3 type of examination, this is specifically based upon the work a group of children have been doing.

The CSE has suffered from a comparison with the General Certificate of Education as there has been an attempt to equate the grades in each when really two different concepts are concerned. This is accentuated by the same children often being encouraged to sit the same subject in both examinations, the philosophy being that, if they fail one, they will pass the other. Such practices are bound to have an adverse effect upon the CSE in that teachers who draw up the syllabuses and examination papers may well be tempted to emulate the GCE pattern. CSE could stand in its own right, though, as an examination of equal status but of a different nature to GCE. As such its relevance to team teaching is obvious. This has recently been underlined by the willingness of several CSE Boards to award more than one certificate for success in an integrated scheme of work.

[1]   See Schools Council Working Papers: *Science and the Young School Leaver, Raising the School Leaving Age* and *Society and the Young School Leaver.*

Opposition to team teaching

These are the main areas within which the technique is likely to be practised. In each the needs of the children are different and team teaching is re-structured to meet these needs. It is not the restrictive straightjacket that some teachers imagine, but enormously versatile. Although flexibility is a good thing in itself, it has often caused team teaching to be harnessed to the most intransigent forms of school organization which, in turn, has brought the technique itself into disrepute. This suspicion of inflexibility is the chief cause of opposition. There are others.

If the scheme cuts across subject divisions some of the staff will probably express concern over the loss of the academic disciplines. Complaints will be heard that the geographical, historical, or religious skills, seen as so valuable for a child's development, will be lost. Others will be uneasy at the complex organizational structures that at first sight appear to be required. There may be anxiety as to the numbers of pupils taking part, that mixed-ability teaching will almost certainly be involved, or over an imagined loss of status. Some teachers may believe themselves unable to work alongside colleagues in a joint venture of this kind, and there will always be the rugged individualist who objects, as he objects to everything suggested.

All these reservations are very real and they must be taken seriously. Unless this is done and they are faced up to, any team-teaching venture is likely to be still-born. Each stage in the planning has to be clear and open to discussion. Preparation needs to be meticulous and the inception of the scheme handled with enormous tact and care.

Initial planning

Having satisfied himself that the type of team teaching envisaged is suitable to the level and area of the curriculum in which it is to be presented, the headmaster must now ensure that space, man- power, and equipment are all suitably utilized. Too hurried an approach must be avoided at all costs. Team teaching is not a technique that can be introduced overnight and so a good deal of preparation is required beforehand. Frequent meetings and much informal discussion will be needed for team members to get to know one another really well. In the initial stages of planning these will probably be of three broad types: the weekly meeting of all teachers in the team to discuss progress in general; a heads-of-department meeting taking place about once a month and dealing with matters of time-tabling, staffing, and future developments; and working parties, which are established from time to time and charged with various functions such as examination in detail of parts of the course, drawing up of objective tests for the scheme, or visiting and reporting back on work being done elsewhere in the area.

As has been said, this might be the pattern at the outset. Meetings of the first and third kind will probably be continued throughout the scheme, but as the subjects merge more fully into one another and initial problems are resolved, heads-of-department meetings may no longer be considered necessary.

The central item in team meetings will undoubtedly be the syllabus itself. Whereas working parties and sub-committees can be established to investigate other matters, this has to be corporately resolved. It will be a decision peculiar to each individual school, involving as it does a range of factors and circumstances of a purely local nature.

Generalization, then, is difficult. One can only refer back to the dominant features of team teaching – a reorientation of the total teaching situation with the needs of the pupils and the unique contribution of each member of staff more directly in mind. It follows that a lot will have to be known about the pupils. Their needs, in fact, can be summarized under four main headings: 'individual'; 'corporate'; 'universal'; and 'social'.

Team teaching may deal with large numbers of children. It may place them in new groupings more suitable to the work in hand, much emphasis might be placed on audio-visual equipment to stimulate interest or present the material in a memorable way, and organization will certainly have to be mechanical in its precision. In all this, though, one thing must never be lost sight of – the important relationship between teacher and individual learner. Most schemes ensure that this is structured in from the outset by placing each child in direct contact with at least one teacher with whom he is familiar and who knows his problems, and retaining this contact as the pupil moves up the school. The teacher's role is that of assisting development along the lines laid down by nature; of encouraging the attainment of latent potential without placing a ceiling upon expectation. It is not one of directing energies into preconceived or artificially contrived channels, and the relationship should not be of the kind that strangles initiative or deters responsibility. This is far more than a 'tutorial responsibility' on the part of the teacher; it is a key factor in the learning situation itself. In the lower part of the school especially, grouping may differ in size and composition; there may be changes in approach, personnel, and numbers as the work proceeds, but the nurturing of personal growth and the meeting of individual needs are factors which team teaching recognizes.

The corporate nature of each group is also of importance, and this is especially the case if the 'class' remains as a basic unit within the scheme. Each group of children has its own special potential and its own unique requirements. These are by-products of the interaction of all the personalities concerned, and cannot really be adduced objectively or until the children have worked together for some time.

Thirdly, there are certain basic or 'universal' needs. These relate to the skills without which the individual cannot realize his innate potential or make any great contribution to the work as a whole. They include skills such as numeracy, written and oral communication, reading ability, and so on.

Finally, there are the needs which have been termed 'social' – the ability to mix freely with others, co-operation and tolerance, tact and understanding. Needs such as these are met in team teaching through the organization of the work itself (see pages 76–81).

Buildings and equipment

From here team planning branches out to take into account details sometimes forgotten. It has to. Unfamiliar groupings of children are to be created; classrooms used in unusual ways. Nothing can be left to chance.

A large hall or assembly room will be required for lead lessons, whilst it is helpful if the classrooms to be used for the follow-up work are adjacent to it and to one another. This eliminates too much disturbance of other classes as the children collect for the large group presentations. The proximity of these classes one to another also allows for temporary interchange of teachers and equipment during the follow-up periods if necessary, or quick exchanges of view between team members. Chairs may not be available in the hall which is to be used. Where are they to come from? The children could bring them with them – not really a good idea on account of the delay and general disruption it causes – or the room can be set out beforehand. This presupposes that it will not be in regular use. It is also good strategy to know exactly what else the children may need to bring with them by way of books or writing equipment.

Quite often the school buildings themselves dictate a certain form of organization, or preclude others. Obviously, the number of children taking part in a lead lesson will be related to the size of the room used. The time-tabling of this lesson similarly depends upon its availability. If the children have to come to lead lessons from all parts of the school, worse still actually go through rooms in which lessons are in progress, the lead lesson is better scheduled to cover the whole of one period. It must begin and end promptly. As will later be seen, this is far from the ideal length although generalizations are again difficult. To a large extent it also negates one of team teaching's attractions – the tailoring of the teaching situation to suit staff and pupils concerned.

Unscheduled or irregular uses of the hall must also be taken into account – the showing of films, ad hoc 'assemblies' of all kinds, conferences or school entertainments. Its use for morning assembly may mean a delayed start of lead lessons scheduled for the first period, its use for school meals necessitate a termination of sessions at definite prescribed times, its housing of the school television make it needed at times not corresponding to those on the time-table.

The type of lead lesson will be defined to a great extent by the positioning and nature of the facilities available. Choral-speaking in the assembly hall next to the headmaster's study is not likely to endear team teaching to him, nor can large numbers of children be expected to concentrate in an ill-ventilated, over-crowded atmosphere. The presence of a stage would suggest that some form of drama might well be structured into the large group presentation, whilst the number and type of power points, and efficiency of the black-out prescribe the range of audio-visual equipment to be used.

This equipment, together with all teaching aids, requires a similar scrutiny. Does it match up to the teaching facilities available, or can it be made to? Will the blackboard be seen by the children at the back during a lead lesson? If not, will projected visual material suffice? Better still, can the school afford an over-head projector? A certain picture may be just the one required for such a lead lesson, but much too small to be seen by two hundred children. Why not photograph it, mount it as a slide, and then project it on to a screen? An epidiascope is very useful for this purpose, but extremely heavy and cumbersome.

The exact range and potential of each item must be explored. A filmstrip, for instance, may present a vivid account of trade unionism, but the sequence be unsuitable for the third-year group. They might understand it better were the strip cut up into individual frames and re-mounted as slides. These could then be shown in an order better suited to the group and the teacher's particular methods. Individually mounted and correctly cata-logued, frames acquired in this way can now be included in the team's collection to be used on later occasions in widely varied lead lessons. A programme on India, for example, can be quickly and successfully produced using slides originating as history, geography, art, and religious filmstrips.

Individual pieces of equipment often have a special contri-bution to make to the work in hand. How can this contribution be best achieved? Your science master may be an expert on photo-synthesis – really good because he knows exactly how to get his material across to younger children. There may also be a visually marvellous film spoilt by too technical a commentary. Can't the two be combined, with the film being run silently whilst the resident 'expert' provides the commentary? Similarly, sections of a film may be shown at a lead lesson, others left out. It is quite common for members of different religious denominations to take part in lead lessons, presenting complementary or opposing views on such matters as 'birth control', 'church unity', 'communism and Christianity', etc. Sometimes this sort of approach is a great success. Often, however, the results are time-consuming and not always to the point. By use of the tape-recorder their opinions may be gathered beforehand, carefully edited, and played back in conjunction with slides. The arguments will still be there, but they will present a coherent whole and will have been specifically adapted with the needs of the group in mind. The speakers con-cerned may then, at a later stage, be invited to attend a lead lesson or smaller session in person, to answer questions arising out of what they have said.

These are the kinds of questions which will have to be asked about buildings and equipment before any team-teaching scheme can be introduced. It is at the planning stage that this must be done. Once a programme is underway other problems tend to dominate thinking and, in any case, it is often far too late for regret or implementation. Several of the points raised may seem trivial. They are not. It is a neglect of minor points such as these that can wreck the most promising of projects. Regard for the finer points of planning, on the other hand, can free the mind to deal with more important detail when the time comes, and quite often opens up new areas of experimentation.

The developmental factor

The developmental factor must also be kept in mind. It would be a mistake to think that very sophisticated forms of organization can take root immediately. Again, this takes time. Time will be needed for a group of individual teachers to begin to work together as a team. No amount of preparation, or attendance at conferences, can do this. Advanced planning can provide the framework within which such development can take place, but expertise at team-work comes only through working in a team. Time is also needed to learn the very different use of the equipment hinted at above and described more fully in chapter seven. The children will require time to settle down under what may well develop into an increasingly free and responsive atmosphere. Time will be needed for team teaching to evolve along lines determined by type of school, personalities of the staff concerned, and local conditions. It can take anything between three and five years before team teaching becomes firmly established in any school. The wise course, then, is to introduce the technique slowly but progressively, making a start in one area of the curriculum and allowing it to spread naturally to others. To rush the organization of complex schemes is to jeapordize the whole.

Sources of inception

In all this it has been assumed that pressure for the introduction of team teaching will come from the staff. The headmaster himself may plant the first seed of the idea, or inception stem from various other sources. A visiting 'adviser' or HMI may be responsible. The idea might come from an in-service training course, a teachers' conference, or the local curriculum development centre. Team teaching may be featured in one of the professional journals or in a television programme, and reach the school in this way. Promotion might bring to the staff someone who has worked under such a system. The possibilities and variations are numerous.

The one way it should not come about, though, is by compulsion. It is easy enough to introduce team teaching in this way, the headmaster honestly believing that his staff will appreciate the benefits once they have worked under such a system. The point is that there can be no benefits unless team members have faith in what they are doing. If this is not the case, attention is unlikely to be given to appropriate forms of organization or preparation, the results nearly always being disastrous. The co-operation of those concerned is essential.

Variety of form

A final point to bear in mind at the beginning of any team-teaching venture is that there is no one set way of organizing the technique. This should be very clear from the brief summary of areas in which team teaching can flourish, given at the beginning of this chapter. An incalculable variation of factors are involved – area, premises, equipment, materials, personalities, experience, attitude, curricular tradition, and so on. Each 'team' is therefore different, and each school will develop its own particular brand of team teaching. This, however, does not detract from the value or importance of advance planning based upon the three factors outlined in chapter one. The diagram on page 20 can now be taken a stage further.

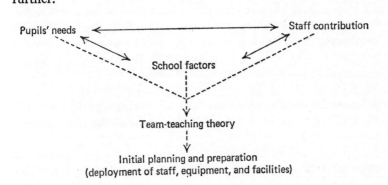

Summary

It will be said that quite a lot of the details described in this chapter can be implemented without team teaching having to take place. So they can. It is significant, though, that they have as yet played no large part in the organization of our schools (see, however the time-table model reproduced opposite). Only when a concerted effort is made by the staff as a whole, or a large section of it, to define objectives and to subordinate all elements to these ends can such reforms come about. 'Team teaching' is the title given to one such effort.

Further reading

Several articles, describing how team teaching was first introduced and organized in schools of various kinds, have appeared in print. They provide invaluable assistance for those in the initial stages of planning such a scheme themselves.

Art and Craft Education, for example, devoted a whole issue – August 1969 – to team teaching, as did *Higher Education Journal* (Spring 1967) and the January 1970 edition of the Catholic journal *The Sower* concentrated exclusively on the place of religious education in an integrated syllabus.

My own article 'Team teaching in a Comprehensive' appeared in *Where*, February 1968, and should be read in conjunction with 'The Henbury File' by T. Rollings and N. Fitton (*New Education*, December 1965) and C. Hanam's article in the December 1965 edition of this magazine. There is also a full description of another such scheme in *An Experiment in Team Teaching* (University of Exeter Institute of Education 1968), whilst J. H. Parry describes the introduction of the technique to his school in 'Framework for the First Year' (*Trends in Education*, July 1968). The problem of introducing team-work is dealt with in two articles in *Ideas* – 'Starting I.D.E.' (February 1967) and 'Starting and Supporting a Project' (February 1969) by L. A. Smith. Two other articles of general interest are 'Strategy for Spontaneity' by H. W. Bland (*Education*, 16th May 1969) and 'Team Teaching with the Remedial Streams' by E. Fearn and M. A. Riley (*Educational Development*, Autumn 1966).

It has already been noted that team teaching originated in many instances to bridge the gap between school and society;

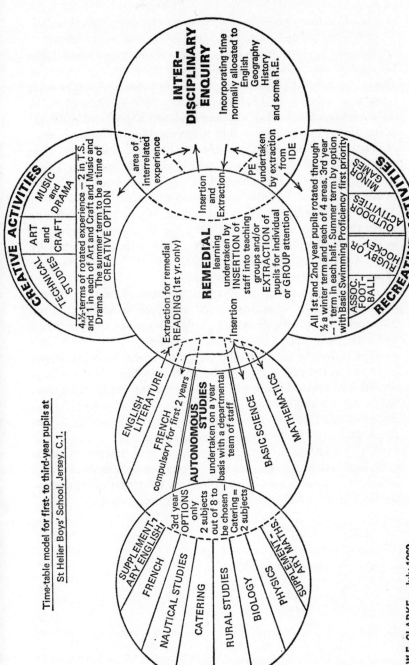

Time-table model for first- to third-year pupils at St Helier Boys' School, Jersey, C.1.

INTER–DISCIPLINARY ENQUIRY

Incorporating time normally allocated to English Geography History and some R.E.

CREATIVE ACTIVITIES

TECHNICAL STUDIES | ART and CRAFT | MUSIC and DRAMA

4 x ½-terms of rotated experience — 2 in T.S. and 1 in each of Art and Craft and Music and Drama. The summer term to be a time of CREATIVE OPTION

area of interrelated experience

Insertion and Extraction

PE undertaken by extraction from IDE

REMEDIAL

learning undertaken by INSERTION of staff into teaching groups and/or EXTRACTION of pupils for individual or GROUP attention

Extraction for remedial READING (1st yr. only)

Insertion

RECREATIVE ACTIVITIES

ASSOC. FOOT-BALL | RUGBY OR HOCKEY | OUTDOOR ACTIVITIES | MINOR GAMES

All 1st and 2nd year pupils rotated through ½ a winter term and each of 4 areas. 3rd year — 1 term in each half. Summer term by option with Basic Swimming Proficiency first priority

ENGLISH LITERATURE

FRENCH compulsory for first 2 years

AUTONOMOUS STUDIES

undertaken on a year basis with a departmental team of staff

BASIC SCIENCE

MATHEMATICS

SUPPLEMENTARY ENGLISH

FRENCH

NAUTICAL STUDIES

CATERING

RURAL STUDIES

BIOLOGY

PHYSICS

SUPPLEMENTARY MATHS.

3rd year OPTIONS only 2 subjects out of 8 to be chosen = Catering = 2 subjects

© W.F. CLARKE — July 1969

to provide a more realistic education for the early school leaver. An excellent and fully annotated account of one such scheme is given in D. B. Boothman's book *Topical* (Longmans, 1967). Miss Boothman has followed up this publication with a series of *Topical Workbooks* (Longmans) for use in schools. Another such scheme is detailed in *Teaching from Strength* by Worrall *et al.* (Hamish Hamilton, 1969), and *The Wybourn Experiment* by W. H. Bland gives an account of how team-teaching techniques were originated and built up in one school over a period of years. This pamphlet is published privately and is available from Mr Bland at 43 Brook House Hill, Sheffield S10 3TB. A book about this whole problem, but related to religious education, is Sir Richard Acland's *Curriculum or Life?* (Gollancz, 1966). Other publications worth reading are – *Education and the Young School Leaver* edited by A. E. Mason (Goldsmiths College, 1966), *All Their Future* by R. G. Cave (Penguin, 1968), and the Schools Council 'Working Papers' already mentioned in the text.

Information about the CSE can be obtained from the Board administering the examination for the area concerned. Some indications of specific aims and objectives are usually published and each year papers, instruction on moderation procedure, and analysis of results are available, for example the Southern Board publishes a first-rate pamphlet *Integrated Studies* which contains several accounts of team teaching schemes in operation in its area. Other publications include – *The C S E* by G. E. Whalley (University of Leeds Institute of Education, 1969) and *Secondary School Examinations* by G. Bruce (Pergamon, 1969).

The relationship between the theory and practice of curricular innovation in general is considered in a collection of essays by leading educationalists, edited by J. F. Kerr, and called *Changing the Curriculum* (University of London Press, 1968).

4. *Patterns of team-work*

'Schools usually have one thing in
common – they are institutions of
today run on the principles of
yesterday.'

Fifteen-year-old girl

Emphasis has so far been laid upon the essential prerequisites of
team teaching. These are – an understanding of its basic tenets,
some knowledge of what may be achieved by its introduction, a
thorough preparation of buildings, equipment, and materials, and
adequate planning of the syllabus and staffing arrangements.
Areas in which the technique can be used have been indicated; the
versatility of the approach stressed. But there has to be a basic
framework within which team teaching can operate, and the
organizational pattern has to be suited to this variety of approaches
and conditions.

Fundamentally there are four types of pattern – the
'thematic'; the 'concurrent'; the 'sequential'; and the 'concentric'.
These can be implemented either within individual subject
departments or when team teaching cuts across such barriers. The
unilateral approach will, by nature, be confined to large com-
prehensives, or the bigger departments of the conventional
secondary school. Possibilities here have already been explored
and, from this point onwards, it is the interdisciplinary approach
that will mainly concern us. This chapter will, in fact, deal
primarily with methods of structuring the co-operation of various
academic departments into a team-teaching scheme.

The thematic approach

The first of the four patterns mentioned above takes its name from
a very general theme running throughout the work. This theme
might be fairly abstract – 'Power', 'War and peace', 'Autumn', etc.

It might, on the other hand, have a strong factual content – 'The voyages of discovery', 'Our community', or 'The coastline of Britain'.

Stemming from this theme are a series of linked topics. 'The coastline of Britain', for example, might be sub-divided into units of work, or 'programmes', such as 'Geographical features', 'Its role in our history', and 'How Christianity came to these islands' (i.e. Augustine, Patrick, Colomba). The whole year group will study each of these topics in turn, so that their actual presentation may well take the form of a large lead lesson and follow-up work suited to the needs of the pupils and the nature of the material. Each unit of work will last for a certain number of weeks, after which a new unit – based on the next 'topic' – will be introduced. The relationship between all these topics may become clear as the scheme progresses. Alternatively, the only link may be through the basic theme from which each unit stems.

The possibilities of this approach will become apparent if the treatment of a single theme is followed through. The one chosen, for example, may be 'The elements', and the subjects contributing towards its study may be science, geography, history, and religious education. Meetings of all teachers taking part in the project will be held and, as a result of these, four topics decided upon. Their titles might be 'The Composition of Our World', 'Formation of the Earth', 'Man Explores His Environment', and 'Man Interprets His World'. These will correspond to a broadly scientific, geographical, historical, and religious treatment respectively.

It may be decided to devote one nine-week programme to each topic, which gives the following basic pattern.

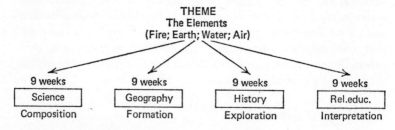

THEME
The Elements
(Fire; Earth; Water; Air)

9 weeks	9 weeks	9 weeks	9 weeks
Science	Geography	History	Rel.educ.
Composition	Formation	Exploration	Interpretation

Smaller groups, or 'teams' of teachers, agree to handle each programme. Staff may be drawn from any of the four contributing departments, but their treatment of the material will be predominantly scientific, historical, geographical, or religious, according to the topic with which they are concerned. The way in which each group of teachers now handles their assignment will depend upon the format and composition of that group.

At planning stage there will still have to be regular meetings of the complete team – say once a fortnight – so that everyone will know how the scheme as a whole is progressing, and to ensure that there is no unecessary duplication of material or treatment. At these meetings the combined experience of teachers drawn from one whole area of the curriculum can be invaluable. It can also prove helpful to invite staff from departments not included in the scheme. This allows the concepts under discussion to permeate throughout the school; ensures that everyone who wishes to knows about developments currently taking place; and may even bring offers of help from unexpected quarters. Much of the subject-matter in the scheme now being considered is, for example, ideal raw material for the English and Art Departments.

Once the work is underway these regular meetings must continue in order to facilitate 'feed-back' of pupils' reactions to each section of the scheme.

It is not possible to generalize about the exact subject-matter of each topic. The more obvious content of each, however, can be surmised. Under the title 'Composition of Our World', the science team will probably wish to deal with the life-giving properties of the atmosphere and earth, whilst water and fire could be taken as symbols of potential and kinetic energy respectively. Power and its various uses may well form the second part of their nine-week programme. Geography's treatment of its topic 'Formation of the Earth' will almost certainly centre around land-formation (earth) and climate (air). The effects of both water (seas, rivers, etc.) and fire (volcanoes, earthquakes, geysers, etc.) upon both are self-evident. Historians thinking about 'Man Explores His Environment' may well wish to include the opening up of continents by men such as Livingstone and Cook, and the exploration of inhospitable regions by others like Scott. The voyages of discovery, recent attempts to sail single-handed around the world, or the importance of the sea to 'this sceptred isle' are also possibilities. Under 'fire' inventions such as gunpowder, the steam locomotive, and rocketry may be considered, whilst 'air' might suggest a treatment of how man has taken 'the wings of the morning'. Religious education's part in this is far more ethereal,

and is rightly reserved to the end of the scheme. It serves to form
a commentary upon the whole, relates it back to the overall
theme, and brings the project to a natural conclusion. 'Earth' will
quite naturally suggest some discussion of the creation of our
world, its nature, and the way we make use of our natural 'gifts'.
'Fire' and 'water' are both Biblical symbols for the power and
presence of God. The relevance of this power to our daily lives
may be raised, or the continued use and value of symbolism in
both secular and religious life demonstrated. 'Air' might well be
taken as a starting-point for examining changing concepts of
'heaven', ancient and modern.

An objection to this approach is the length of time devoted
to each topic. Nine weeks represents a sizeable portion of the term
and there may be anxiety that, once science has completed its
topic, it will not be heard of again throughout the year. This
difficulty should not arise as each programme will contain follow-
up work relating to all four disciplines. A more direct way of over-
coming the difficulty is to schedule eight smaller topics of five
weeks duration and to let the subjects alternate as shown here.

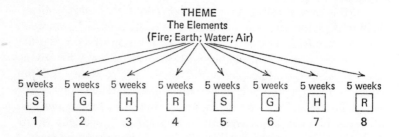

The content of these topics might now become – 1 Science:
Composition of Earth and Atmosphere; 2 Geography: Land For-
mation, Seas, Oceans; 3 History: Invention and Discovery, Land
and Sea; 4 Religious Education: Earth and Air – Man and His
Spirit; 5 Science: Power and its Uses; 6 Geography: Natural
Forces; 7 History: Man Harnesses Power, Air and Space; 8
Religious Education: Uses and Abuses of Power.

Subject integration

Another drawback to this approach is the lack of relationship
between individual topics. This can be overcome if subject

departments are prepared to integrate more fully with one another in such a scheme of work. If, for example, the same theme is taken, but a more dynamic sub-title – 'Man's Conquest of His World' – substituted, each individual 'element' can form a separate topic in itself. The topics will, however, be closely linked and transition from one to another may well pass unnoticed, as this pattern shows.

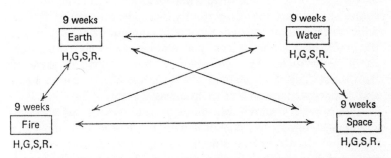

THEME
The Elements
(Man's conquest of his world)

9 weeks — Earth — H,G,S,R.

9 weeks — Water — H,G,S,R.

9 weeks — Fire — H,G,S,R.

9 weeks — Space — H,G,S,R.

Once again it is difficult to speculate about content of individual topics. Variations here are greater still. An examination of a part of just one of these topics, however, will suffice to show how close and rewarding the integration of subjects can be.

The topic loosely entitled 'Earth', for instance, has great possibilities. In his perennial quest for supremacy and knowledge mankind has had to overcome many barriers. Desert, jungle, arctic waste, river swamp, underdeveloped areas, wild-life of all kinds, the destructive forces of nature, germs, disease, parasite, over-population, incorrect use of soil – all these and many more have been contended with. But nowhere can this ceaseless struggle be so imaginatively captured than in our conquest of the great mountain ranges. This facet of the larger contest can, in turn, be vividly symbolized by the Ascent of Everest in 1953. Sir John Hunt's expedition of that year could well form a dramatic opening to an investigation of this whole area of human experience.

In an investigation of this kind the subject skills concerned would be combined in such a way that they could not rationally be separated. An understanding of geography is needed to set the scene generally and place it in its context. Knowledge of different kinds of mountains, their formation, geographical importance, and ease with which each type can be scaled will be helpful. Changes in vegetation as the ascent is made will also need to be known, as will the reasons for these changes. Mountains in general also have a significance of a more spiritual nature. They have always featured largely in the development of religion; in some areas of India they are venerated as holy in themselves. What would be the effect upon the superstitious mind of this challenge of the eternal by the spirit of transitory and 'scientific' man?

A third area of significance that mountain ranges have can only be described as historical. They form the boundaries of some countries; they protect others from attack. The Himalayas allowed Tibet to remain an isolated, theocratic community for centuries; the cradle of a unique culture and religion. Even now this range would seem to be the main obstacle to a Chinese invasion of South-east Asia. It is one of the frontiers where communism and democracy face each other in uneasy truce.

Historical research can unearth the records of previous attempts at the ascent, and deal with the narrative of the 1953 expedition. It will not be able to do so, however, without some understanding of the difficulties involved. As has been seen, these are partly geographical, partly religious, but chiefly scientific. Everest could not have been climbed until the atmosphere at high levels had been successfully compensated for, until communication had been greatly improved, or until artificially heated clothing developed. Similarly, the geographical part of the work cannot proceed without the assistance of science in an understanding of such factors as soil composition, air pressure related to height, and the causes of volcanic eruption.

The recording of all this information requires mathematical skills on the part of the children. They will need to be able to draw graphs and transfer contours into three-dimensional images. The narrative will stir their imagination so that, for some, creative writing (the 'feel' of an excess of oxygen; the 'sensation' of being first to stand on 'the roof of the world', etc.) will result. For others, descriptive prose and poetry will be more appropriate, whilst pure narrative, drama or mime ('Invasion of the Yeti!'; 'What We Saw from the Top', etc.) will be the end-product. Others will wish to express such concepts visually. English, art, and mathematics are three other disciplines that could be incorporated into the scheme throughout.

Concurrent themes

The organizational pattern that has been termed 'concurrent' is really an extension of the thematic approach. In this case, though, two or more themes are in operation together with the same group of children. The Art Department may wish to run a course on 'Impressionistic art' whilst the Music Department plans a series of lessons on 'Impressionistic music'; the Maths Department may decide to complement a geographical study of 'Rainfall and temperature' with one of its own on 'Graphs'.

In cases such as these each course could be run on independent yet parallel lines, having continual cross-reference and links with each other. But there is much to be gained in both these cases from an even closer liaison. Exchanges of classes and the joint use of equipment and materials could be arranged, whilst independence of theme and subject autonomy guaranteed.

To take the music/art example cited above, programmes could be organized in this kind of a sequence.

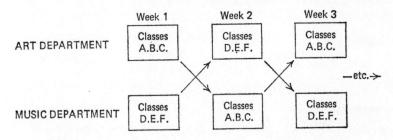

In this way two teams of teachers will concurrently be at work with the same group of children and classes will alternate between the two either on a weekly or a fortnightly basis. The work they do may consist of the normal kind of approach adopted in each subject, or the lead-lesson/follow-up framework may be decided upon. Arrangements like this may be short term ones, as the geography/maths link-up mentioned above, or they could last throughout the school year.

An alternative arrangement is to run each series of programmes for half a term, or half a year, and then to switch groupings. This is far less complex and also does not require so much co-operation between the two teams. It is therefore suitable for themes which are related but not closely linked, such as 'The

Industries of Britain' (geography) and 'The Industrial Revolution' (history), as shown here.

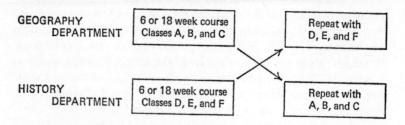

Special circumstances may require the running of three separate themes concurrently. As well as the two examples given above, the English Department may wish to add a third element, independent yet related – 'Industry in Literature' – which will include authors such as Charles Dickens, D. H. Lawrence, Arnold Bennett, and John Braine. This can be organized so that each subject takes one third of the total time available to develop its theme, or in the following way.

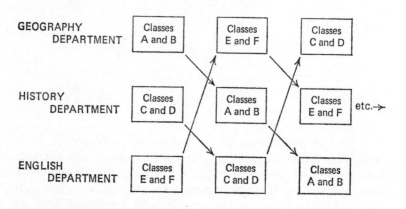

The cumulative sequence

Another way of organizing the contributions of various departments to a team-teaching scheme could be called the 'cumulative sequence'. Here no 'theme' is presented to the pupils at the outset, but an overall pattern is built up as the work proceeds. Programmes are linked consecutively, rather like beads on a necklace, but their relevance to other programmes in the sequence does not become apparent until the final phase of the scheme. This makes the approach more suitable for older or more academic pupils, but it can be adapted for use with younger children, as indicated below, if its handling is skilful and imaginative.

The subject departments taking part may be geography, history, and religious education. Thirty-six weeks can be regarded as a fairly average school year, and this is divided into six sections of six weeks each. The preparation of material will be by teams consisting of members of all three departments, but each of the departments will have supervision of material presented in two of the six-week programmes.

The History Department may begin the scheme with the Anglo-Saxons, out of which will emerge the 'Coming of Christianity to England' (R.E.). This terminates with Norman and Angevin church building in villages throughout the country. At this point history comes in again with a programme on the mediaeval village, after which the Geography Department has something to say on land utilization past and present, illustrated with a series of 'sample studies'. The church in the local area (R.E.) may follow this, and geography concludes the year's work with further sample studies and a treatment of urbanization. This would lead naturally into the following year's sequence, commencing with an historical programme on the growth of towns, producing this pattern.

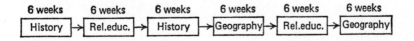

6 weeks	6 weeks	6 weeks	6 weeks	6 weeks	6 weeks
History	Rel.educ.	History	Geography	Rel.educ.	Geography

The concentric pattern

The team-teaching pattern that has been called 'concentric' is frequently used with the young school leaver. A closely integrated approach is called for, indeed the subject disciplines as we know them hardly enter into it. The pupil, something he knows very well, or an institution to which he belongs, forms the starting-point. From here the syllabus radiates outwards and can be related at any point to the daily life or corporate existence of the pupils concerned. Thus the first programme may be simply called 'Me', and deal with such matters as the physical working of the body, general statistics relevant to the age-group, opinion polls, and group findings on matters such as how much money is earned each week, how it is spent, hobbies, sports, and pastimes. This programme could be scheduled to run for two weeks. Thereafter, short programmes of one to five weeks' duration could deal with a progressively widening range of topics – My parents; My neighbours; My work; My money; My marriage; My home; My children. Another concentric approach could deal with communities – School community; Local community; Town/village community; Communication; Communities past; Communities far; Religious communities. Yet another might deal with – This motor bike; Its manufacture; Its servicing; Its licence and insurance; Its driver and his safety; Its dangers and possibilities; Its maintenance.

The pattern, then, is like this.

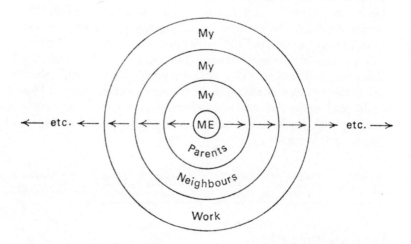

Individual programmes

Schemes such as these will provide a framework within which the year's work can be organized. Their planning and implementation will be the responsibility of the whole team. Each individual programme within the overall pattern, though, will also need careful planning. As has been seen, this will probably be the task of a smaller group of teachers, and unless some thought is devoted to the work at this level there will be no cohesion within the whole. It is this aspect of team teaching that must now be considered.

Further reading

A general exploration of this whole area is made by Miss E. Richardson in *The Environment of Learning* (Nelson, 1967), in P. Rance's *Teaching by Topics* (Ward Lock, 1968), in *Opportunities for Learning within a Flexible Timetable* (University of Exeter Institute of Education, 1968), in 'Open Education' by R. S. Barth (in *Educational Philosophy and Theory*, October 1969), and in Charity James's article entitled 'Flexible Groupings in the Secondary School Curriculum' in *Education for Democracy* (Penguin, 1970, pp. 154–60).

Two interesting articles are – 'Experiments in Theme Teaching' by B. Jones and M. Horne (*Forum*, Summer 1966, pp. 96–99) and 'Experiments in Team Teaching' by Miss J. Clough (*Times Educational Supplement*, 7th February, 1969). This kind of approach is also dealt with in *Enquiry and Experiment in the Comprehensive School* by D. Holly (Comprehensive Schools' Committee, 1968).

The use of the environment of the school and the neighbourhood often feature largely in such schemes. Two books of interest here are *Learning Through the Environment* by M. F. S. Hopkins (Longmans, 1969) and *Environmental Studies* by D. G. Watts (Routledge and Kegan Paul, 1969).

5. *Programming the work*

'Excitement should be injected into
school, so that one is completely
surrounded by and part of it.'

Ann, 18

All the approaches to team teaching mentioned in the last chapter
are based upon the division of the year into a series of interdisciplinary or integrated programmes. These are related in length
and treatment to the children and material concerned. A programme on 'Coal', for example, will probably not last more than
two weeks; one on 'The voyages of discovery' may well take five
or six. Again, the last topic will take longer with young children, who will need to explore the imaginative possibilities and
assimilate concepts by means of models, diagrams, charts, and
paintings.

The organization of each programme will largely depend on
some form of lead lesson, given to numbers appropriate to its
nature and treatment, the equipment to be used, the classroom
scheduled, and the children for whom it is intended. This will be
supplemented by follow-up work with smaller groups under the
supervision of a member of the team. Lead lesson and follow-up
work are two basic concepts of team teaching.

The lead lesson

The basic idea of the lead lesson is that it shall stimulate interest
and capture the imagination. The following week's work largely
depends upon it, so it must have impact, drive, and variety. To
ensure this a wide range of techniques and teaching-aids need to
be used – film, filmstrip, slides, tape-recorders, back projections,
visiting speakers, exhibitions, outside visits, to say nothing of the
personality of the teacher or teachers responsible for its production.
The lead lesson also serves as a 'key' presentation, bringing together

the full group, or a large section of it, ensuring continuity and, if necessary, providing direction.

It is important to relate the type of approach to the material which is to be presented, and thought also needs to be given to an appropriate sequence within the 'lead'. Is it better, for example, to begin on a dramatic note – say, the Battle of Hastings – and then trace the events leading up to it, or to give a straightforward chronological treatment? Does one describe the climatic features of Argentina and then ask the children to note the effect on the clothing, houses, and farming to be seen in a series of slides, or do the slides themselves come first before the children are asked to deduce these factors from them?

Each different situation will require a different arrangement of the material. Whichever sequence is decided upon, though, the main features of the lead lesson must be agreed upon, and there should not be more than four or five of these in a twenty minute session. It is far more effective to concentrate upon a few key issues which can be vividly illustrated than to overload the lead lesson with too much material.

It is quite common for two or more teachers to present a lead lesson jointly. This, in turn, opens up new possibilities, and experimentation should be encouraged. Will each teacher be concerned for one section of the lesson, or is a 'duologue' possible? Should unanimity be preserved in front of the children, or would a variety of opposing views be more appropriate? Can one teacher be responsible for the blackboard work, whilst another deals with the projector, and a third handles the lesson itself? In large groupings to what extent can the children be involved? What form should this participation take?

Certainly the pupils should be more than passive spectators. Their involvement is important and can be engineered in several ways. Spot questions can bring individuals into the work – especially if it is known that the person concerned has something to contribute at a certain point in the proceedings. This usually proves extremely popular with younger children and, if the questions are of an 'open-ended' type, the approach can be fruitful at all levels.

The taking of notes is appropriate only with older and more academic classes. Even here it should be introduced only after considerable practice has familiarized the pupils with the principles concerned. Brief headings on the blackboard or by means of an overhead projector will keep the developing pattern in the children's minds, whilst duplicated sheets are sometimes given out at the beginning of lead lessons for this purpose. Another method is to provide sheets which need to be completed during or directly after the 'lead'. Perhaps a sketch has to be made from the slides of sheep being sheared, or a two-minute description of a rift valley written. A simple questionnaire may also serve to focus attention on a specific problem at the outset, whilst diagrams to be completed or labelled during the course of the lesson are in frequent use.

It is generally a good idea at any level to tell the classes which question is going to be asked, or which points raised, before the showing of a film or series of slides. 'At the end of this lesson I am going to ask you why the two kingdoms divided at the death of Solomon. You should be able to discover five reasons in the next twenty minutes'; or – 'Make a note of as many defensive features as you can during this film on the Norman Castle'; or – 'We will see how many of you can apply these principles to the central heating system on a house when I have finished'. Individuals should not be embarrassed by forced participation in what, to some, could easily become an ordeal. On the other hand, a feeling of joint participation in the learning process should be actively encouraged.

Lead lessons usually take something under one period of forty minutes, the time varying with the age and concentration of the children, but it is useful to have a double period blocked into the time-table when it is to take place. This enables teachers to begin follow-up work while the material is still fresh in the children's minds. Conventionally, lead lessons take place once a week and are given to any number up to about two hundred at a time. the standard procedure in a six form-entry school is illustrated opposite.

As can be seen, the lead lesson is given twice, to about 120 children on each occasion. For schools wishing to experiment with two alternative kinds of approach this, of course, is ideal.

Varieties of lead lesson

Variety is one of the essential features of the lead lesson. This is not likely to be maintained if the same format and presentation is always used. If, each week, the children are asked to listen to two

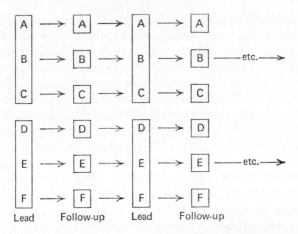

teachers giving a talk backed up with slide or filmstrip the approach is bound to pall, however brilliantly it is done. Nor will changes to presentations of the same basic nature suffice. Film with either taped commentary or teacher's comments is, for example, too close a replica of the original. Entirely new patterns need to be introduced; pure routine avoided at all costs.

If it is necessary to get a lot of information across and much of this can be presented visually, an exhibition can be mounted. Here classes might be prepared beforehand for what they are going to see, possibly have work-sheets which direct their attention to several broad areas of the display. One or two classes can visit the exhibition at a time and collect information or gather ideas for use during the following week. Outside visits can also take the place of the lead lesson, being organized along similar lines. The emphasis here becomes not 'What will teacher tell us about Chepstow Castle or the Imperial War Museum', but 'What can we find out for ourselves using the brief outline provided'?

A very good example of just this was the occasion when I and other members of a team had taken a group of first year children on just such a visit to Avebury. On the way back we passed two mediaeval grinding stones outside a public house. The coach was stopped and the children treated to a brief yet brilliant three-minute dissertation upon this from the history master. They listened intently. At the end, a hand went up and a small group of about four children told us, very politely, just how wrong we were. They had not made any of the assumptions that we had. In fact, they had actually been in to see the landlord who informed them that the 'flour mill' was really a cider-press and that, in the Middle Ages, the whole village used to turn out to man the press. Not only had these children used a certain amount of initiative. Far more. For them – and for everyone else on that coach – the bulk of the information painfully learnt over ten years of schooling will be forgotten within a few months of leaving it. But I doubt whether to their dying day any one of them will forget the afternoon the coach stopped and three of their number gave 'Sir' a lesson in his own subject! The more of this kind of 'teaching' that can be structured into our educational system the better. It is because I know that certain forms of team teaching give the time and opportunity for it to happen that I advocate it so strenuously.

Other variations on the standard lead lesson and follow-up are the visiting speaker or speakers, a forum of the staff, a display from the Schools' Museum Service, or a 'Press Conference' where, for instance, the headmaster is quizzed on various aspects of the school rules.

Forms of organization

It must not be taken for granted that two large groupings will always be retained for a repetition of the same lead lesson. It has been said that two different approaches might be experimented with, and to continue to long in the same routine is doubtful practice. This can lead to undue familiarity with the technique on the part of both staff and pupils, culminating in tedium. Different ways of combining classes or variety of organization need to be considered.

The complete year group can be taken on visits to large areas, such as the Yorkshire Moors, Tintern Abbey, or Avebury. Exhibitions, demonstrations, and experimentation will probably require two classes rather than three scheduled together for the lead lesson. This form of organization may also be dictated by the size of the classroom to be used, the type of equipment available, or inflexible time-tabling. With it will come increased time for the follow-up work, and this must be taken into account when planning such an approach. The basic pattern now is shown at the top of the opposite page.

Alternatively, if the problem is a lack of time rather than space and equipment, it may be decided to schedule four classes together for the lead lesson. This does place an added burden upon

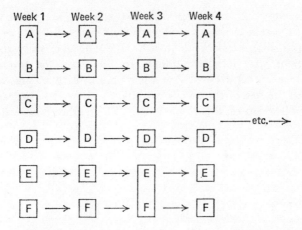

those responsible for presenting the material, and it gives rather heavy weighting to the 'lead' element in the total scheme. Very careful thought has to be given as to whether the merits of the project outweigh its organizational complexities. One of the advantages, though, is that children are more likely to be taught alongside all members of their year-group under this approach, as can be seen here.

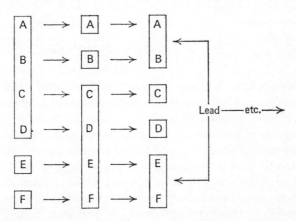

Perhaps mention should here be made of an understandably rare method of team teaching that can take place within subject departments. It may be that the departmental head wishes to make contact with all the children in a particular year group, that one of his staff has something special to offer to the term's work, that a special piece of equipment is to be used, or that the head of

T.T.—5

department is the only experienced teacher in his subject (frequently the case in religious education!). One of these factors may be coupled with a lack of adequate facilities, or an unwillingness to experiment with large groupings. In this case, the teacher or equipment concerned will visit each class in turn to present the material, the rest of the term's work being devoted to preparation for, or follow-up of, this single lesson. The pattern is shown here.

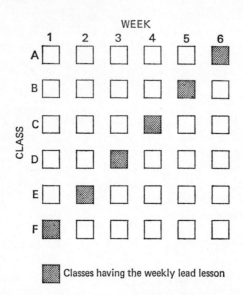

Classes having the weekly lead lesson

It is doubtful if the process, as described here, matches up to the criteria of team teaching outlined in the opening chapters. However, if the single lesson which is repeated to each class in turn is given by someone from a different subject department, it becomes more rational. There is far more to be said for it if, for example, a thread on the Islamic and Christian religions supplied by the R.E. Department was to run throughout a history course on the Crusades. It would be even more worthwhile if to this could be added a third element – a geographical treatment of the Middle East. This would not be too difficult to plan, the one man single-period lead lessons being introduced as shown opposite.

The assumption in all this has been that lead lessons will occur once a week. This need not be the case. They can be scheduled once a fortnight, once a month, or need not take place regularly at all. Flexibility is essential. To obtain this a combination

WEEK

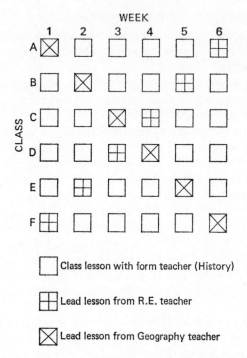

Class lesson with form teacher (History)

Lead lesson from R.E. teacher

Lead lesson from Geography teacher

of all the approaches already described, together with any pertaining to the special circumstances of each particular school, must be used. Organization and approach, though, should as always be related to the needs of the pupils and the material in hand.

Follow-up work

So far it has also been assumed that follow-up work will take place within the conventional framework of classes or forms. Under this kind of organization, each team member is responsible for a group of about thirty-six children. Sometimes he is involved in the presentation of the lead lesson, in which case he will know the material intimately. On the occasions when others are taking the 'lead', he will attend it with his class, take his own notes, and be provided well in advance with a duplicated list of text-books available and suggestions as to how the lead lesson might be followed up. He is then free to deal with the material in any way he wishes as long as he keeps within the broad framework provided by those responsible for that particular part of the course. The group will probably work together on this material, the teacher reporting back to the weekly meeting regarding the progress made and the children's reactions.

Alternatively, the children may be placed into smaller groupings according to their interests or various aptitudes. The size of these groups will be determined by the kind of work they are to do. Large groups of fifteen or twenty children can work together on projects such as an investigation into the design and purpose of the parish church. An interview with the vicar and preparation of the subsequent report will not occupy more than two or three pupils. Model making or research in the library are suited to groups of about five; up to ten children might be concerned in accurately mapping the school grounds; the whole of a normal class could be involved in drama or mime. Once these groups have been formed the children may work individually on a similar task, or be jointly concerned in a group project. One teacher will be responsible for the supervision of several such small groupings.

Follow-up work is just as important as the lead lesson and adequate time must be given to it. Maximum benefit will not be derived from the 'lead' unless this is so, and the scheme will be considerably weakened. An average of three to five follow-up periods are necessary each week. The first of these should, ideally, come directly after the lead lesson to enable immediate re-capitulation of the material and a running through of the work schedule for the week. It is therefore helpful if the lead lesson can be time-tabled for the beginning of a double-period. This allows for such immediate follow-up and, if the rooms where this takes place are nearby, permits the lead to continue for longer than forty minutes if necessary.

Team teaching, then, can be viewed as a process which may be presented diagramatically in the way shown opposite.

It consists of a broad general direction of energies in successive lead lessons, and the incorporation of individual talents in the follow-up work. Interaction between the two occurs with the stimulation of activity brought about by the lead lesson and the modification of future 'leads' in the light of the children's response. Freedom of activity can thus be ensured within a broad framework; directional flow established. Both are ultimately in the hands of the team responsible for the planning and implementation of the

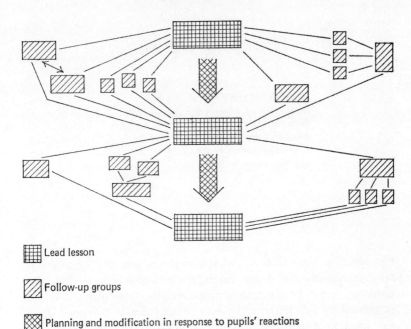

▦ Lead lesson

▨ Follow-up groups

▧ Planning and modification in response to pupils' reactions

Team teaching in England: a diagrammatic representation

scheme. In this way team teaching allows practising teachers to take a more direct part in curricular revision.

For further reading

Most of the books and articles included at the end of Chapter Four are also appropriate to this chapter. To them can be added *The School as an Organization* by P. W. Musgrove (Macmillan, 1969), *Teaching, Communication, and Learning* by L. S. Powell (Pitman, 1969), *School Organization* by T. I. Davies (Penguin, 1969) and *Education in Focus* by E. C. D. Stanford (Religious Education Press, 1965).

6. Grouping the children

'Respect for the pupil is just as
important as respect for the teacher,
because after a young person's opinion
has been disregarded three or four
times the young person may never
express an opinion again.'

Sheila, 15

An overall pattern of the kind traced in the last two chapters is
very necessary for team teaching's success. Some thought,
however, must be given to appropriate groupings of the children
suggested by this pattern. To some extent this will depend upon
the level at which team teaching is to take place and the area in
which it is to operate, but at all levels and in all areas of the curriculum one general principle should be followed – size and
composition of group must reflect content and nature of the material.

It will be remembered that this material, which forms a syllabus
for the scheme, was originally derived from the needs of the pupils,
the contribution to be made by the staff concerned, and circumstances peculiar to each particular school. All three factors, but
more especially the first and second, must also be kept in mind
when grouping the children for follow-up work.

This brings our cumulative diagram of a team-teaching
scheme into its next phase (see diagram opposite).

Types of academic organization

As the complete curriculum is unlikely to be geared to team
teaching in any one year, existing academic structures are important. The policy of 'streaming' may be practised. In other words,
children are grouped by ability into classes upon entry, given the
material and approach relevant to the group in which they find
themselves, and are moved up the school in these parallel units.
If they fail to come up to the required standard of the stream in

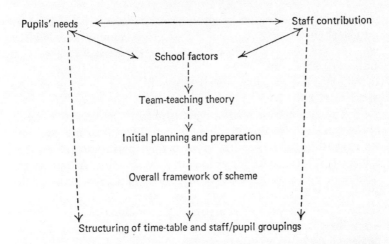

Pupils' needs → Staff contribution

School factors

Team-teaching theory

Initial planning and preparation

Overall framework of scheme

Structuring of time-table and staff/pupil groupings

which they have been placed, or if they prove worthy of more intellectually stimulating treatment, they are correspondingly moved up or down to another class.

'Setting' is frequently introduced in the middle or upper secondary school as specialization becomes more important. This is a system of streaming within individual subjects. Thus a pupil may be in a top 'set' for maths, a middle one for history, and the bottom 'set' for English. As English and maths usually feature largely in deciding to which stream a child has hitherto been allocated, this particular case would present problems to any headmaster. Setting eases these problems and ensures that real ability in any one area – say music or modern languages – is recognized. This might not be the case when streaming is in operation as weakness in other fields could well place the individual in a low general group for all subjects.

Another form of academic organization is known as 'broad band streaming'. Here the year's intake is streamed in the usual way but, in order to alleviate the dangers of too rigid and inflexible compartmentalization, two or three adjacent streams are linked. In a nine-form entry school this might be the 'A', 'B', and 'C' streams, the 'D', 'E', and 'F' streams, and the 'G' and 'H' streams. Class 'I' in this case might well be regarded as the remedial form. These groups of classes are now seen as 'bands' stretching across the whole curriculum. They study the same subjects, are taught by the same staff, and transition between classes within them is easy.

Finally, a school may make no such assumptions about its pupils' ability or the way it will develop in years to come. Children will be allocated to classes either in a haphazard fashion (i.e. alphabetically or on the basis of the primary school from which they have come) or, more probably, a deliberate attempt will be made to mix the general abilities of those within each class.

The reasons for such a departure from traditional practice are recent findings that children tend to live up to the concepts we have of them. Regardless of what their norm was before, it is said that 'A' stream children inevitably react with 'A' ratings for behaviour and attitude, that 'C' and 'D' streams soon take on the characteristics associated with such classes. It has also been claimed that this process is assisted by a similar streaming of staff – the 'best' teachers are allocated to the 'bright' forms, the rest having to make do with what is then left.

On the positive side the claim is that children learn very quickly from those about them. Placed in a low form with other 'slow learners' there is little chance that the environment will be conducive to learning. In fact evidence is mounting up to show that it is overwhelmingly the children from a poor environment who find their way into such classes. There is no 'compensatory education' about this; no hope of the school making up in some way for earlier deficiencies. The final argument for non-streaming relates to the 'late developer'. It is pointed out that once children are streamed at the age of 11-plus, the possibilities of moving out of that particular track through the curriculum become progressively more remote. Rates of progress differ, different subjects are taught in different streams, set-books, texts, and equipment all vary to an increasing extent.

Team teaching's role

These, then, are the different forms of academic organization that may already be in existence within the school.

Team teaching can be adapted to suit any of them but, before this step is taken, it might be as well if careful thought is given to exactly how each of these caters for the needs of the children and the contribution to be made by the staff. Are the needs of the less academic child really served by placing him in a class composed entirely of fellow slow learners? In this situation will his levels of aspiration ever be raised beyond those of the lowest common denominator? Just as success breeds success for the able pupil, will this be achieved at the price of failure begetting failure lower down the school?

Alternatively, is it fair to the gifted child to put him in a group where his talents might be severely restricted? Will the individual receive sufficient attention under the system of streaming or setting, geared as they inevitably are to the class working as a unit and to a set syllabus? And the teacher – if the school is un-streamed, how can he cope with classes of thirty-six children comprising a multiplicity of talent and levels of intellect?

As has been said, team teaching can operate within any one of these systems, although its nature will differ slightly with each. In a streamed school the lead lesson can be used as stimuli for two or more of the contiguous classes concerned, which then return for follow-up work geared to their respective streams. The technique is especially suited where broad banding has been adopted, as the large groupings for the lead-lessons already form part of the academic structure. Setting presents more of a problem. Team teaching can be introduced here but, unless the 'concurrent' approach (see page 55) is used, it is difficult to see how more than one subject can take part. Mixed-ability grouping presents no problems; indeed, it is probably the type of organization most suited to teamwork.

Team learning

This suitability is partly due to the technique – a lead lesson which sparks off interests and enthusiasms of all kinds, and then structures these repsonses into the scheme by way of activity-centred follow-up work. To divide children into streams or sets might seem to imply that some of these responses were of a secondary nature; that the more acceptable forms of reaction come from those classes labelled 'A' and 'B'. Worse still, it could imply a streaming of the staff, as already mentioned.

It is accepted that some children's responses to the material will be mainly 'academic', that some will react in a more imaginative sort of way, whilst follow-up work for others will have a 'practical' bias. Under streaming and setting such aptitudes are likely to be segregated – the 'A' stream being academic, the practical approach being relegated to the third or fourth division. All these ways of treating the material, though, are really complementary and need to be seen as such. Aspects of each approach should be practised in each classroom, and mixed-ability grouping is the most likely form of organization to ensure this.

The suitability of unstreaming for team teaching is also partly due to a concern for the pupils' interest. As has been seen, levels of aspiration need to be raised in any school as respect for others can only emerge from an initial respect for oneself. This is also important because of the emphasis placed upon co-operative work in many such schemes. The name 'team teaching' implies co-operation among the staff. 'Team learning', however, should also be a part of the whole process. The question still remains – how can mixed-ability work and, with it, 'team learning' be organized?

A rational basis for this whole approach would seem to be recognition of the fact that children are a subtle mixture of many different 'abilities'. These 'abilities' and 'aptitudes' have to be seen as equal in importance for the child, if not for us. They must be given parity of esteem. It is totally unreasonable to condescend to admire a fine piece of model-making, but to demonstrate by one's every action that skill in, say, English or mathematics is regarded as far more worthwhile. Children, especially young children, will not understand this, and a rejection of the things at which they are really talented will be interpreted as failure and any attempt to channel these energies into other directions will be resented. This, of course, is exactly what has been done in the past to so many of the pupils in our schools – the 'slow learners', the 'remedial stream', 'Newsom children' – call them what you will! Society has chosen to place emphasis upon one or more selected skills and has segregated children in accordance with this decision, first into schools, and later into streams within those schools. All this means very little to the children and it can be maintained, with some justification, that society has been the loser through it.

Streaming, or grouping by ability, often achieves only two things for the majority. It destroys much of the innate potential of the individual; it places emphasis upon competition rather than a co-operative pooling of resources and experience. Failure, rather than success, is structured into the system from the very beginning.

Attainment of innate potential, a pooling of talents, and personal self-esteem through successfully making information one's own are three objectives shared by many educational innovations in recent years. Team teaching is just one of these innovations. It provides a stimulus in the lead lesson. Work of this kind is given further impetus by a closer association in follow-up work between pupil and teacher, and in a different kind of relationship between the two. Follow-up work has been described as either taking place within conventional classes or in interest-centred groups. This whole process of structuring in the talents and enthusiasm of the children – basing the whole upon achievement – is still further assisted by the way each unstreamed class is organized or each mixed-ability group handled.

Some approaches to unstreaming

Faced with a mixed ability group for the first time, teachers seem to adopt one of four different approaches.

Some choose to ignore the possibilities of unstreaming and continue to teach their classes in exactly the same way as they always have done. Some of these teachers are fortunate and able to carry it through on personality alone, but the majority find that old, well-tried methods – ones that have achieved magnificent results in the past – just do not seem to be working any more. At this stage it is easy to blame the system; to say that this is what happens when idealism is given its head, or that mixed-ability grouping can never work. Possibly most of the opposition to unstreaming comes from this quarter – or from those who have never tried it.

Another common approach is to form groups of like-ability within the class. So, in point of fact, one has an 'A' group, a 'B' group, a 'C' group and so on, within the class itself. The labels might not be there, but no one is taken in! This is streaming exacerbated by being conducted within the confines of the classroom. If adopted, the benefits of unstreaming are marginal.

Sometimes lessons are continued in the normal sort of way until difficulties are encountered by the slow learners. These are then withdrawn from the main group and given remedial help whilst the rest mark time academically with exercises or text-book reading. As the former come to understand the work, so they are fed back into the class. One group slowly increases in size, the other decreases. Frustration is experienced all round. The children in the large group feel they are being held back, and those in the group of decreasing size feel guilty because of this and get even more confused, the teacher – strung between both groups – is soon worn to a shred!

The last of the four approaches seems to be far more realistic. It does not represent grouping for mere convenience, or as an end in itself, as the other three might almost appear to be. Here it is used as a method of harnessing a variety of aptitudes, abilities, and experience for the common good. It takes account of the purpose of mixed-ability teaching and lends itself to some exciting and varied approaches. In essence it is the formation of groups not by ability or haphazardly, but by a careful balancing of the different abilities and personalities concerned. The children, as well as the teacher, must know exactly why they are there – 'Peter is with you because he is good at writing'; 'Angela always gets on well with people, she will do some interviewing for you'; 'I wish I could draw and sketch like Tony – that's why he is here'.

Structuring in success

This kind of approach is far more positive than the others. It begins with something that can be achieved and works outwards from this point. Each child, although working together on some joint project, is really making a unique and individual contribution to the whole. Success in some aspect of the work is the starting-point; co-operation between a series of such 'successes' the basis of such grouping.

If follow-up work is conducted within a form or class, the children can be organized along these lines by the teacher concerned. If, however, it is decided that the whole venture should be run co-operatively the total year group may be so divided, with appropriately sized groups tackling each different aspect of the study. In either case it will be found that the kind of approach here indicated may well bring about radical changes in overall framework and organization.

The theme being studied may be, for example, 'The Middle Ages', and the staff drawn from the history, geography, English, and religious education departments. Following a stimulating lead lesson, open to many different interpretations and dealing with a variety of aspects of life at this time, each class will decide to concentrate on one 'topic' within the whole. One of them may choose 'The Mediaeval village', for example, another 'The Town', a third 'Monasteries', a fourth 'Crusades', class five may select 'Farming', and class six 'Fairs and travel'. Topics should not be duplicated if possible, which may mean that a list of all the topics that can be handled – given the material and staffing available – has to be made. Teachers may make the choice for their class, although it would be more in keeping with the general approach if the children were allowed to do this.

The pattern, then, differs from other kinds of team-teaching ventures that have been described, as we see here.

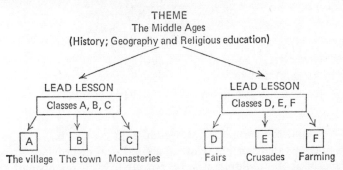

THEME
The Middle Ages
(History; Geography and Religious education)

LEAD LESSON — Classes A, B, C
A — The village
B — The town
C — Monasteries

LEAD LESSON — Classes D, E, F
D — Fairs
E — Crusades
F — Farming

If the scheme is introduced at the beginning of the school year and links have not yet been formed between individual teachers and classes or groups, staff now choose the topics in which they feel most confidence. 'Monasteries' and 'Crusades' would be obvious choices for the R.E. teacher, 'Towns' and 'Villages' for historians, 'Farming' for the geographers. Should such an allocation of staff prove difficult, follow-up work under the direction of any member of the team is made possible by a careful preparation of materials, books, and equipment. This will have to be done well in advance of the project in any case.

Each class will now divide its topic under sub-headings. The topic 'The Mediaeval village', for instance, may be subdivided into 'The manor', 'The land', 'The church', 'Fairs and travel', 'Trades and occupation', 'Costumes and armour'.

It will be seen that here the various subjects in the scheme are all actively involved in its implementation.

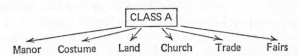

CLASS A

Manor Costume Land Church Trade Fairs

In a class of thirty-six children, groups of six will be allocated as previously described to each sub-topic. Thus, within each small group, a variety of approaches will be adopted. Sketches will be made, accounts written, models constructed, local sources discovered, interviews recorded, drawings completed, drama and mime prepared, research carried out, and so on.

The emerging picture, then, is as follows:

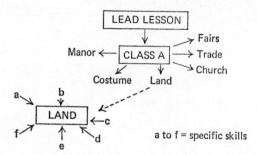

Should the complete year group split on this basis without any previous division into classes, a good deal of previous knowledge about the children will be required. Each member of the team is now responsible for the composition and supervision of several such groupings, and the size of each will largely depend upon the nature of the work undertaken. Whichever approach is decided upon, the teacher's role is as important as that of his colleague within a conventionally organized classroom, but the nature of that role very different.

The role of the teacher

Once a project is underway the teacher acts in an advisory capacity. He knows what material and equipment is available and where various pieces of information can be obtained. Careful planning has ensured this. He also has up-to-date knowledge of what each group is doing and can thus direct discussion or research if difficulties are being met, and possibly temporarily merge two or more groups when this would seem beneficial. Individuals may be withdrawn for consultation with other groups and, at times, all units need drawing together for a semi-formal lesson.

The teacher's task here is also one of widening each individual's horizon. Using initial achievement, which is ensured by careful grouping, each pupil must now be actively encouraged to take a step outside his 'specialization', be it drawing, modelling, writing, research, etc. This may prove difficult at first, but as each child finds that not only is he an active member of a small 'team', but also that the results of his work are actually being incorporated into its findings, the effects are usually extremely gratifying.

A breakthrough here can quite often be engineered by organizing a small classroom exhibition at the end of a set period of time, say four or five weeks. In this way not only is all the work done drawn together for the benefit of the complete class, or a number of the groups, but each pupil can actually see the contribution he is making towards the whole. Tony's detailed sketch of the plough is there next to Peter's written description of the three-field system, whilst Angela's taped interview with the keeper of the local museum complements both. The model of the manor is placed alongside pictures of the costumes worn by those who lived in it. A vivid account of the siege of Berkeley Castle, sketches of siege-engines of the children's own design, and a carefully re-constructed mime on knighthood and the oath of fealty, all form one unit, distinct yet linked with the rest.

When the contribution that the individual has to make is positively emphasized in all these ways, the results are sometimes startling. Not only does the standard of his special 'ability' improve, but quite often his whole attitude and behaviour as well. Having gained self-respect, he can now treat others as individuals to be respected. His work in other fields often slowly progresses, and he can now be persuaded to enhance his model by the addition of short cogent sentences, or paragraphs describing its main features or how it was constructed. The importance of mathematical accuracy can be recognized when it relates to his precise piece of work. More care is taken over labelling and presentation; ideas for improvement are readily forthcoming.

It is one of the joys of this kind of work that it is, to a large extent, self-perpetuating. The children can see it taking shape before them; they have a positive hand in its direction. All are working towards a common goal, and upon the strength and weakness of their combined efforts it will ultimately succeed or fail. Responsibility for this is shared by all – pupils and teachers alike.

The slow learner and the gifted child

The position of the slower child under such an approach has been made clear. His levels of aspiration are not lowered to reflect those associated with one of the bottom streams, and his real interests are made the starting-points for a more positive approach to the work. Sub-consciously he will be learning from those around him, whilst the value he comes to place upon his own contribution may well be mirrored in a newly won self-esteem.

The place occupied by the gifted child in all this might cause some concern. What about his aspirations? Won't he be terribly restricted in such a group? Is he to be sacrificed for the good of the whole?

It can be maintained that it is in a streamed situation that this child is going to be held back. Normally he will be reduced to the pace of the slowest, for it is the essence of class teaching that all shall progress at a uniform rate. But in an unstreamed situation, upon completion of his part of the project, he will be engaged in the library or elsewhere on further research of an advanced nature. Not only this but he will have the duty of returning to the group and presenting his findings to them in a lucid form. Information obtained in this way and the requisite re-interpretation of it for the group ensures really sound learning of a type he is unlikely to meet elsewhere. Besides this, the very able child is brought into close contact with pupils he might otherwise never meet so that he begins, in many cases, to appreciate their problems, to sympathize with their difficulties. This can only be for the good both in the immediate situation and in future life.

Secondary stimulation

Mention has already been made of small classroom exhibitions, mounted in order to bring each topic to the attention of all groups. But each class or group is here studying 'The Middle Ages' in its entirety, and not just one specific aspect of the period. There, therefore, has to be an interchange of ideas and material between them. This could take the form of visits by children to one another's exhibitions, or possibly a large display of the work done by the entire year-group in the hall. Such an exhibition would very definitely be functional by nature, and not merely publicity for the scheme, or 'window-dressing' for a parents' evening. Prior consideration would be given to an arrangement of the material so that the children are helped to learn more about the central theme. Work-cards or sheets might direct their attention to certain aspects of the exhibition, larger issues for consideration arise out of it, or direction to local sources could be given. The exhibition will, in effect, serve as a secondary stimulus, reviewing each group's interest and throwing fresh light upon their work viewed in the context of the total picture.

Another method of secondary stimulation well worth experimenting with is the lead lesson given by members of staff but based on the material collected by the children. Some attempt could be made to get groups to describe what they have been doing during the five or six weeks of their research. This kind of approach is good in the classroom, and in all probability will form part of the follow-up work, but the children are not professionally trained to handle up to two hundred others of their own age, nor do they have the authority or personality to master such a situation. The teacher, on the other hand, has both the training and the skill. A series of lead lessons arising directly out of the children's work and using material from the exhibition achieves several ends. Firstly, as has been said, this will act as a secondary stimulus to the whole project. It will also stress the importance of the children's own researches. A skilfully handled lead lesson will be an exposition of how to arrange and edit material, and of the difference added emphasis upon certain parts of it can have. Stress will also be placed in this way upon the concept of teacher and children working together in a joint enterprise. The pattern may be this:

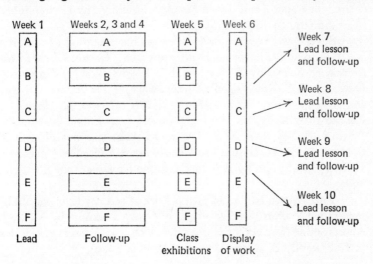

This whole approach can be viewed as a series of 'teams' that overlap, interchange, form, and re-form as the scheme progresses. There is the original team of teachers who come together to plan and prepare the project; there is the year's intake, working together upon many aspects of one 'theme'. A third team can be said to be the teacher and his class, or the series of groups under his supervision, and finally there is each small group of children. They, too, are a 'team' in their own right.

Further reading

Standard works on streaming: *Streaming in the Primary School* by J. C. B. Lunn (NFER 1970), *Streaming – An Education System in Miniature* by B. Jackson (Routledge and Kegan Paul, 1964), *Education and the Working Class* by B. Jackson and D. Marsden (Penguin, 1966), *Social Relationships in the Secondary School* by B. Hargreaves (Routledge and Kegan Paul, 1966) and *Social Class in the Comprehensive School* by J. Ford (Routledge and Kegan Paul, 1969). Two special supplements to the magazine *Where* – 'The Flexible School' (No. 5, 1965) and 'The Unstreamed Comprehensive School' (No. 12, 1968) deal quite fully with the theory and practice of unstreaming, as do many issues of *Forum*.

The teacher's role in such a situation is described in the pamphlet *Teaching in the Unstreamed Secondary School* (University of Exeter Institute of Education), 'Collaborative Group Teaching' (*Ideas*, June 1968), and 'Open Minded Teaching' by L. Stenhouse (*New Society*, 24 July, 1969).

Several works are now in print on the grouping of children and the organization of such an approach: *Group Work in the Secondary School* by B. Kaye and I. Rogers (Oxford University Press, 1968), E. Richardson's *Group Study for Teachers* (Routledge and Kegan Paul, 1967), *Mixed Ability Groups in Secondary Education* by R. W. Seckington (University of Exeter Institute of Education), *New Roles for the Learner* by A. E. Mason (Goldsmiths' College, 1967), H. Entwistle's *Child-centred Education* (Methuen, 1970) and B. Simon's article in *Education for Democracy* (Penguin, 1969).

Finally, two studies of group work at tertiary level should be mentioned – *Aims and Techniques of Group Teaching* by M. L. J. Abercrombie (Society for Higher Research, 1970) and *Participation in Learning* by B. King (Allen and Unwin, 1970).

7. *Materials and equipment*

> 'Nobody can be greatly inspired by
> . . . the boring, antique, blackboard-
> and-book methods.'
>
> *Richard, 17*

In recent years tremendous interest has been shown in the production of teaching materials for use in the classroom. Several of the Schools Council schemes have centred around this aspect of curricular revision (see page 17), teachers' centres in many parts of the country have held evening 'workshops' for the production of such material and mounted exhibitions of the work achieved, whilst commercial firms have not been slow in realizing the potential of such developments. The results of all this activity are a range of items which, five years ago, were completely unkown outside the walls of a few progressive classrooms. Resource packs, teaching kits, item banking equipment, teaching machines, educational games, simulation exercises, orienteering apparatus, are all now available on the open market.

Self-help and adaptation

The avowed aim of bodies such as the Schools Council and the Nuffield Foundation is to put into the teachers' hands material which is not only of great intrinsic worth but will also require a re-thinking of classroom method and procedure before it can be effectively utilized. With the emphasis very much upon discovery techniques, an approach through a variety of interests or skills, group-work, individual re-interpretation, and the making of information one's own, this whole philosophy accords perfectly with the spirit of team teaching as outlined in earlier chapters. Not only are new materials to hand which can help with the development of such schemes but, possibly of greater importance, is what can be gleaned from them about the adaptation of existing school stock. New items will obviously have to be purchased as team teaching is progressively introduced into a school. However, a good deal of self-help should also be encouraged. It is in the thinking about and the construction of such teaching aids that so much of their value lies whilst, given new direction or used in different ways, materials and equipment which the school already possesses can also be effectively used. When this begins to happen – when teachers create their own materials to meet the developing needs brought about by team-work, and when they think of adapting existing stock to this end – one of team-teaching's aims is achieved. Our 'aids' have ceased to be our masters and are once more brought to serve the purpose for which they were initially devised.

The problem, then, is twofold – that of knowing the kind of materials that will support and enrich team-teaching schemes such as those already described, and the adaptation of existing stock towards these ends. Whilst the use of any one item in isolation is not advocated, a start can be made with the traditional tool of the teacher – the text-book.

Text-books and library

Under team teaching there will be little use for the standard texts covering a wide range of material and used year after year by classes in the same kind of way. Nor will the books used be allocated to pupils for retention throughout the term. Texts, on say, 'England, 1485–1666', 'Israel from Wilderness to Exile', or 'The Geography of South-East Asia', will not normally be used or, if they are, will be reserved for the school or classroom library. More desirable are smaller sets of vividly written, well illustrated booklets that go into far more detail on topics such as 'The Slave Trade', 'An Australian Sheep Farm', 'Seed Dispersal', 'The Maccabaean Revolt', or 'Mathematical Sets'. These can be used in a variety of ways. In themselves they form the basis of a project for an individual, a group, or a class; passages, photographs, diagrams and such like within them can be referred to in passing; together they can be used to cover the material of a more traditional text-book. Treatment of the material in these books needs to be fairly open-ended, lending itself to various approaches, raising points for discussion, or directing attention to possible local evidence for the material in question. There are several such series on the market at the moment and a welcome addition to them are the growing number of folders containing photostats of original documents, discussion sheets, and so on.

These books and folders will probably be needed by several groups of children, and so should be readily available at some central point. A record of where they all are at any given time will probably be necessary to safeguard against copies disappearing without trace, and to ensure that they can be found in an emergency. It can be extremely frustrating to know exactly where to look for a diagram or piece of description you require but unable to use it because no one knows where to find any of the fifteen copies of the book in question.

As there are likely to be quite a number of these small booklets or folders available within the joint enterprise, it is a good idea to make a record of all references to certain popular topics within them. Thus there might be an excellent descriptive passage on the Stuart House of Commons in one book, an eye-witness account of the Gunpowder Plot trial in another, a clear picture of the conspirators in one of the folders, and a first-class summary of the effects of the plot in one of the standard works of reference. All these would be entered under one heading, but with cross references to other topics. The school is then well on the way to preparing its own study-folders, or 'rescource packs' upon certain topics.

The school library will prove an important source of information. This, of course, must be well stocked and combine ease of access with availability of information. It will not prove very useful to team teaching if it is used by the school as an extra classroom and so has lessons being conducted in it most of the day. Research at all levels can take place during follow-up periods if the library is free and, for this purpose, two or more pupils must be able to work together. As long as they are conducting a disciplined enquiry, it would seem unwise to insist on complete silence.

Class libraries are also extremely useful in this situation. Reference books of every kind and at every level should be readily available.

Work-cards, work-sheets and questionnaires

Work-cards, work-sheets, and questionnaires will play an important part in the follow-up work. Sometimes they will be used in conjunction with the kind of literature already described, directing the children's attention to books kept in the classroom, in the team's general stock, in the school library, or sometimes in the reference section of the local lending library. Passages may have to be contrasted, diagrams copied or traced, deductions drawn, comparisons made. Above all, work-sheets and cards supplement the great defect of all text-books, however good. The authors of these books cannot know all the areas of the British Isles and, if they did, they could not possibly relate their work to every one of them. They will not know the children who are to use their books personally. Material produced by the school relates the content to the immediate locality ; it directs the children's attention to first-hand examples of everything that has been written. Such material is also prepared with specific children directly in mind. Not only do work-sheets and work-cards refer to books, but are often centred on local churches, museums, and places of interest. In this way the horizon of the classroom is broadened considerably.

It is through work-cards that existing books which might otherwise be unsuitable for team teaching can be adapted. The teacher selects the relevant passages from these books and directs the children's attention to them by carefully worded questions, reinforcing the points made in language more suitable to the needs of the children concerned, and possibly referring them to other books or visual-aids. Here is an example of this, currently being used in a Leicestershire school:

'Ever since men first learned to think they have puzzled about the beginnings of our world, wondering how it was formed and how it developed into the world we know today. This programme will give you some of the answers. You will need to read from pages 4 to 24 only in . . .

1) Our world developed in 'stages', some of which took millions of years, each 'age' or period is given a name. Turn to the back of this book and copy the chart which gives you the names of these ages and tells you how long they lasted. It would be a good idea to make your chart with an extra section (next to events) where you could draw an example of what was developed during that period. The example below will show you how to set this out . . .

9) Page 14. What is the difference between a reptile and a mammal? Look this up in an encyclopedia if you do not know or ask your teacher. What early mammal was like a

dog but developed into something else? This is called evolution and like most of the other information you are learning has only been known for the last 100 years.'[1]

Some schools produce their own booklets for pupils' use in team teaching. These are often divided into sections which accord with each lead lesson and subsequent follow-up work. Either the teachers concerned are very sure that their material is going to be just what is needed, or these are regarded as purely short-term measures. Alterations are likely to be structured into the scheme after each item in a particular programme and inflexible material does not allow this to happen to any great extent. Quite a common practice, though, is to prepare follow-up sheets running to some three or four pages of foolscap in the week preceding each 'lead'. This combines knowledge of the children and material concerned with flexibility needed if last-minute alterations are to be made.

Role of the teachers' centres

The teachers' centres can play an important part in this whole matter of resources and equipment. They are able to bring to the teachers' attention the latest developments in audio-visual aids, to bring in outside experts in various fields to give talks or demonstrations, and many of them open in the evenings and at weekends as practical 'workshops' where units of work can be discussed, planned, and prepared. As a result of this study-kits on a variety of topics are made available to schools in the area as well as valuable experience in their preparation being gained. In some cases sizeable central 'banks' of material have been amassed from many sources, a selection of material on any topic being assembled on request.

Materials for the children's use

For the children's own work, loose-leaf files or folders are far more suitable than the traditional kind of exercise book. The latter makes the tacit assumption that material will be followed through in a certain prescribed order and that, once 'entered up', no further re-arrangement will be necessary. It also rules out the possibility

[1]   We are grateful to Mrs C. Redfearn, Senior Mistress, Brockington High School, Enderby, Leics. for permission to preproduce this extract.

of information discovered at a later date being added to previous material. When involved in a project on the Parish Church, for example, a pupil might find some new evidence about one of the local families he was studying the term before; perhaps an inscription on a tomb or changes in a coat of arms through marriage. Again, some of the information previously written up about local seaside resorts might well have to be revised in the light of current research into changes in population. Both these alterations would be impossible in the normal school exercise book. With loose-leaf files re-arrangement of material, alteration in sequence, and later addition of information are all simple matters.

Files such as these need not be expensive. Their covers are similar to those of a normal exercise book, and they include some form of device so that the loose leaves of paper can be firmly held in place until needing to be removed or re-arranged. Another advantage of the system is that plain paper, sheets ruled for arithmetic, graph sheets, as well as lined paper can all be inserted where necessary. A central stock of all types will need to be kept, and of course existing stocks of exercise books can be used for this purpose if holes are made by a paper-punch. Added durability can be ensured by asking the children to cover their files. Wallpaper samples from out of date stock can easily be obtained from most decorators or hardware stores and these give the files a pleasing appearance. They also add individuality to the uniform sets of files, enabling children to pick out their own work at a glance. Plastic covers are now avaiable from wholesalers or any stationery shop. It may seem trivial to say that files need to be of uniform size, but it is not until one has attempted to transport a set of thirty-six books of all shapes and sizes about a building that one realizes just how infuriating this simple operation can become!

Clip-boards will also prove an essential part of the classroom equipment. Decently produced ones, made of stout wood with strong clips, can be taken anywhere and used as portable writing tables. Psychologically they are effective, too. Striding purposefully along, clip-board under arm, gives most children a real feeling of achievement!

Projectors, slides, and filmstrips

Turning from materials to equipment, a similar variety in range and usages can be seen. Once more it is the pupils and the syllabus that will dictate how audio-visual aids are used rather than the opposite to this, as is sometimes the case.

The cutting up of filmstrips so that their individual frames can be more flexibly used has already been mentioned – this being a classic example of simple yet effective adaptation of existing stock. The individual slides obtained in this way can be used in lead lessons (see page 43) and can also be used in conjunction with those taken by various members of the staff for follow-up work.

Much publicity was recently given to a primary school which received all the projectors and filmstips it required from one of the commercial companies as a 'practical' experiment. The children used the equipment themselves and gained much from it. Few of us will ever experience such munificence, but it should not be forgotten that slide-viewers cost as little as 3/6d (17½p) each, and that cardboard mounts for a filmstrip treated in the way described above run at about 3/9 (19p) for fifty. Half-a-dozen such viewers, a collection of relevant slides and filmstrip frames, pre-recorded tape, work-sheets, and text-books make an extremely effective unit of work for surprisingly little outlay of expenditure.

Here is an example of this technique, again in current use in Leicestershire:

HOUSES AND HOMES

Show the series of slides through first, then discuss amongst yourselves any points of interest you may have noticed, e.g. Do you know a house which resembles any one you have just seen? (for instance, Belgrave Hall in Leicester is identical to slide No. 13). Is your house picture here? – (Perhaps No. 21 or 22?) If money was no object, which house would you choose to live in? . . .

Slides 1 and 2 – Compare the two slides and read the information on pages 4 and 6 of your Ladybird Book. Do a section on each of them, choosing which information you consider most interesting and putting it in your own words. Make sure you explain why the people in the second slide are able to live more comfortably. What extra comforts can you see? Do you know anyone in the world today who makes houses this shape?

Slide 3 – Here you see a beautiful Roman Villa. Do you think it is a suitable house for our climate? Find out all you can about the Romans. What else did they build in England which was entirely new? The Romans lived in Britain and ruled here for 400 years. Find out why they left.'[1]

Slides in a kit like this may be individual frames from one or several film strips, taken by members of the staff in the normal course of events or especially with a specific team-teaching project in mind. The children might also be encouraged to use photography as one of their tools for recording and presenting information. Several cheap 35mm cameras, capable of taking coloured photographs, could be a useful addition to the equipment. All slides and filmstrips, of course, need storing centrally and cataloguing under topics. This could be the task of some of the children concerned with the work.

It is helpful if there is a corner of each room that can be set aside for the individual or group use of the strip-projector. Failing this, part of a corridor or entrance-hall may be set aside for joint use in this way. The projector itself should be adaptable for both slides and film-strips, as most models currently on the market are. If a new one is to be purchased note should be taken of the noise it makes when in operation. Some models drown even the loudest voices, which precludes their use in a large lead lesson. For this purpose the automatic or semi-automatic models may be considered, as well as those which allow the teacher to stand at the front of the room and work the machine by means of a hand control. It almost goes without saying that the plug must correspond to the sockets in each classroom or, that if a variety are in use, suitable adaptors will be needed; that spare bulbs, fuses, and plugs need to be readily available; and that extension leads may also be required.

Some thought needs to be given to the most appropriate use of the filmstrip projector in the lead-lesson. Is there to be a straightforward projection of material of the same basic type? Or will both slides and strip be needed? In this case two projectors will probably be required, mounted side by side. Commentary can be provided by the teacher or teachers concerned, amplified if necessary through a tape-recorder, or use made of pre-recorded

[1] We are grateful to Mrs C. Redfearn, Senior Mistress, Brockington High School, Enderby, Leicester, for permission to reproduce this extract.

material. Appropriate music, sound effects, dramatic interludes, or actual interviews can be incorporated into the treatment in this way. If the required slide is not available, home-made illustrations or diagrams can take its place. There are three ways of providing these. Either an exposed film can be taken and the picture needed scratched on to it by means of a pin or a compass point, or the drawing made on translucent paper with a mapping pen. If there is plenty of time available, the simplest method is the third – the preparation of a clear drawing which is then photographed for projection on to the screen. These three methods are all also ways in which children's work can be incorporated into the 'lead'.

The assumption here is that the original picture will not be large enough to be seen by all the classes in the lead-lesson. One way of producing large diagrams or drawings which can be used in the more conventional way is to project one of the filmstrip frames on to a large sheet of paper and then trace round the outline of the main features of the projected image with a pencil. When removed from the wall this can now be inked in and coloured. The overhead projector can also be used in this way. Many of these machines now have an attachment whereby diagrams or drawings made with chinagraph pencil on cellulose can be projected on to the screen as they are prepared. They are therefore extremely valuable in lead lessons where such an approach is required.

Film, film-loops, and their projectors are not open to nearly such a variety of approaches. It must not be forgotten, though, that the whole feature does not have to be shown. Hired films should, of course, never be cut under any circumstances, but it may be felt that the maximum impact is achieved only be showing one sequence or section. The film is threaded into the projector at this point and just the required piece shown when needed. Commentary by a member of staff is sometimes preferable to that on the actual soundtrack. This improvised commentary can relate the material to either the locality or the needs of the specific children to whom it is being shown, and can be given 'live' or pre-recorded.

Some schools have their own 8mm cameras and projectors. Lead lessons can be based upon such material, but this may prove expensive since the film would have to be shot and edited in a professional sort of way.

The tape recorder

Several references have been made to the tape-recorder and its uses in the lead lesson. Within the classroom it can be used for follow-up work in several different ways – recording group discussions, interviews, local sounds, in conjunction with slides, and so on. Part of the tape leading up to a new phase in the project, setting out various tasks, or leading into a discussion, can be pre-recorded if required. A piece of metal foil can then be stuck to the tape itself where the pre-recorded part ends and, if the recorder has an automatic cut-out device, the children are now able to listen, record, and play back without much danger of accidental erasure. In this respect experimentation with the use of the twin tracks of a four-track machine can prove fruitful.

Another use can be the building up of a symposium of the sound of town or countryside. This can be as important for the classroom as a collection of pictures on a similar theme; indeed, the two can be welded together with interesting results. Such ideas could form the nucleus of a classroom 'sound library'. A bank of material gathered in this way can prove invaluable to those responsible for preparing a variety of lead lessons.

All this will probably require equipment to facilitate editing and preparation of taped material. A quiet 'studio' is unlikely to be part of the original school buildings, but improvisation and adaptation can achieve a lot. I once had to drive my van at frequent intervals into the middle of the school playground when it was not in use and leave the children there to record material for one of the current themes.

C-C T V and programmed learning

Far more sophisticated items include closed circuit television and programmed learning. Not many schools are equipped to use the former which, with its central studio and various receiving points scattered throughout the building, might have been designed with team teaching in mind.

Teaching machines of varied sophistication are having an increased appeal. Basically the programmes used break down learning into easy steps and structure achievement into the system as each is assimilated. The basic assumption is that there is an agreed body of knowledge that has to be put across, and so programmed learning will not be suitable for all team-teaching ventures. However, its value in the building up of basic skills for the individual is important and many machines are so designed that programmes can be prepared for them by teachers within the school. Programmes based upon each unit of work could therefore be prepared by the team if required.

Servants or masters?

All the uses of the audio-visual aids and materials have to be in support of the syllabus agreed by the team, and to meet the needs of the pupils. This is as it should be. It is far too easy to become obsessed with equipment, using it purely for its own sake; forcing both syllabus and children to fit in with its dictates. In this way, too, the personality of the teacher can become submerged behind a battery of such educational 'hardware'. One can think of many examples of both these dangers from everyday experience – classes being withdrawn from their normal work because a 'good' film has arrived at the school, schemes of work being 'bent' to include a certain filmstrip or tape-recording, the teacher opting out of the teaching situation in favour of a series of films or visiting speakers, and so on.

My own personal experience of this is somewhat classic. I once witnessed a list of notes written on cartridge paper, photo-graphed in colour, projected on to a screen, and 120 children being asked to copy them down in the semi-darkness of an overheated hall! In such a situation one might well ask – who was in control, man or machine?

Further reading

There is no shortage of published material on all aspects of this chapter. First, some general books:
Aids to Modern Teaching by R. T. B. Lamb (Pitman, 1967), *Blackboard to Computer* by G. Kent (Ward Lock, 1969), *Mass Media in the Classroom* by B. Firth (Macmillan, 1968), *Modern Teaching Aids* by N. J. Atkinson (McLaren, 1966), *Experiments in Education at Sevenoaks* (Constable Young, 1965). The *New Statesman* article 'The Challenge of New Teaching Techniques' by N. Mackenzie (7 October 1969) is also of interest.

A. Wright's *Designing for Visual Aids* (Studio Vista, 1970) deals with this topic more comprehensively than most, whilst

A. Francombe's *Notes on Photo-Play* (Kodak, 1962) introduces an interesting new concept.

Screen Education Yearbook is an annual which should be available to all team teachers, and valuable information can also be obtained from *Teachers and Television* (Goldsmiths), *Teaching and the Overhead Projector* by J. Schultz (Prentice Hall, 1965), *Teaching with the Tape Recorder* by J. G. Jones (Focal Press, 1962) and *On Tape* by D. N. Wood (Ward Lock, 1969).

Newer developments can be followed through – 'The Place and the Value of Item Banking' by R. E. Ward (*Educational Research*, NFER, February 1968), *Item Banking* by R. Wood and L. S. Skurnil (NFER, 1969), *Simulation and Gaming in Education* by P. Tansey and D. Unwin (Methuen, 1969), 'Theory and Practice of Educational Simulation' by B. Boardman (*Educational Research*, NFER, June 1969), *A Handbook of Programmed Learning* by G. O. McLeith (University of Birmingham, 1964), *Programmed Learning in Schools* by L. Leedham and D. Unwin (Longmans, 1965), *Programmed Learning, its Development and Structure* by P. Callenden (Longmans, 1969), and 'The Organization of a Teachers' Centre' by W. Curry (*Visual Education*, December 1968).

8. The flexible school

'Children live in synthetic fibre houses
and then have to spend half their lives
in dark relics that our age is afraid to
demolish because of the loss of the grasp
with the past. Children have changed,
the schools should!'

Lynda, 16

It is in the nature of things that there is always a lapse in time
between changes in society and their effect upon the curriculum of
a school. Concepts about what should be taught and the principles
involved in teaching it are clearly reflected in the architecture of
the buildings and the arrangement, both internally and externally,
of the classrooms. It follows, then, that today's experiments in
education will largely be conducted in conditions governed by the
beliefs and methods of the late 1950s and early 1960s. Add to this
a perennial reluctance to devote any sizeable portion of the nation's
wealth to schooling below tertiary level, and one has the spectacle
of ventures such as team teaching, integrated studies, mixed-
ability work, and Nuffield Science taking place in cramped and
often dingy surroundings; in schools with narrow corridors,
uniform classrooms often of a rigidly specialized nature, the
children sitting in serried rows of antique desks which cannot be
arranged in any other way, and sometimes, the quaint notion of
separate staffrooms for men and women teachers!

Features such as these may be a legacy from our scholastic
past, but they are also factors mitigating against educational reform
in the present. Just as certain concepts about the curriculum pre-
suppose certain forms of organization, so the existence of buildings
and classrooms designed in accordance with such beliefs will play
a part in perpetuating them. They will – in future years – exert a
conservative or reactionary influence over educational planning,
all the more dangerous because it lies at sub-conscious level.

It follows that the design of any school must be as flexible as possible, allowing for any developments that may take place, indeed, encouraging their growth. This is now realized, and schools such as Wetherby Deighton Gates (see the plan at the back of the book) are built with this in mind. But until most existing buildings are phased out of the system many of us are faced with the prospect of experimentation conducted alongside improvisation or conformity to a bygone norm.

Even if conditions are not as extreme as those described above, the buildings are likely to have been planned on the assumption that groupings would remain constant, that classes would work as a unit, the focal point of all lessons would be the teacher, blackboard, or some visual aid at the front of the room; and that academic disciplines would be catered for in different parts of the school.

Team teaching makes no such assumptions; the needs it creates are far less rigid. These would seem to fall into three categories – those related to the pupils; those related to the staff; and those related to a new use of materials and equipment.

The needs of the pupils

Team teaching infers that the size and composition of the group will be related to the content and nature of the material it is studying. This indicates the necessity for rooms of varying sizes, ranging from small boothes, or carrels, where individual work can be carried out, to large halls capable of holding up to two hundred children. Most schools possess the latter, as Morning Assembly is one of the factors presupposed in the design of any such building. One may also be fortunate enough to have other similar rooms for school meals, house-rooms, lower school functions, and so on. With a little ingenuity these can be converted for lead leasson purposes. On the other hand the one suitable room available may also be used for P.E., drama, or house the school television. In cases such as this the size of any lead lesson has to be reduced or methods of team-work not involving such large groupings adopted.

Some mention has already been made about the prerequisites for a lead lesson (see page 60). The room must comfortably hold the number of children who are to attend it and there must be easy access to chairs. If the acoustics of the room are poor, amplification may be necessary, but the average tape-recorder can be easily adapted for this purpose. All children as well as hearing what is said must be able to see the blackboard or screen, nor must it be forgotten that – from some angles – bad distortion can occur. Adequate blackout is obviously necessary, not the kind that billows out at the slightest breath of wind and causes maximum distraction, but heavy curtains or roller blinds. If the latter are installed perhaps simplicity of operation should be a key factor to consider. More lead lessons than I can remember have been ruined from the outset by hoards of excited children wildly pulling at multifarious snarled ropes.

The room to be used should also have electric sockets suitable for those of the school's audio-visual equipment, and length of flex might have to be supplemented with extension leads. Trolleys with easy running castors are more suitable for the projector than tables or desks. If they are used the equipment can be wheeled into the position required according to the size of the picture needed with the minimum of noise or disturbance.

Ideally, the rooms to be used for the follow-up work need to be adjacent to the hall and to one another. This means that other classes will not be disturbed at the beginning and end of lead lessons and that interchange of staff or pupils is not difficult to arrange. The 'clustering' of rooms around a large hall or 'resource area' is a central feature of many current school designs (see the plans of Hatfield Middle School and Merrywood Comprehensive at the back of the book) whilst in America the problem is being overcome by skilful use of 'walls that move' shown in the plan of classroom 2 in Death Valley High School, on page 98.

Rooms need to be furnished in such a way that they can serve several different purposes as required. Sometimes they will be used as conventional classrooms, with the teacher giving a 'straight' lesson. On the other occasions they will have to be blacked out for the showing of a film or other visual material. The requirements of group-work will also have to be met and so it must be possible for three to fifteen pupils to work together in this way. Individuals or small groups may have to be withdrawn from time to time either for consultation or training in the basic skills. For this purpose it is helpful if there can be a small 'bay' or office situated in or near the classroom. The majority of schools will not have facilities for individual study other than a 'quiet room', to which anyone can go. In most cases this will be the library. However,

Ministry of Education Building Bulletin No. 18

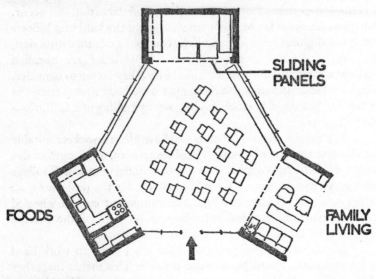

GEN SCIENCE

SLIDING PANELS

FOODS

FAMILY LIVING

CLASSROOM NO. 2

APPROX. AREA EX. BAYS
563 SQ. FT.

3 0   9   18   27 FT.

*A plan of Classroom 2 at Death Valley Union High School,
Shoshone, California*

its use as an alternative classroom or for research of the nature described on page 85 will rule out its use in this way. It may be decided to convert part of a classroom, cloakroom, or corridor for the use of individual pupils, and small booths could be fitted up for this purpose.

A general idea of what a school designed along these lines will look like can be gained from the ground plans of the John Smeaton Comprehensive School Leeds, shown at the back or the book.

Furniture and equipment

Flexibility of this nature will probably be achieved by a wise choice of furniture and equipment. Tables are very useful and serve far more purposes than do the traditional desks. Writing, modelling, and painting can all be successfully done on them, whereas the desk is esentially an aid to written expression only. These tables could be individual ones, but those at which three or four children can sit together are probably more suitable. They are of the correct size for one small group to work on and, when pushed together, must present a smooth surface. Both chairs and tables need to be stackable so that quite a large area can be cleared quickly and with as little confusion as possible.

The kind of classroom furniture described here can be used in several ways according to the nature of the approach adopted. The tables can be arranged in rows for the standard classroom lesson. They can be placed around the room and sat on during a 'theatre in the round' or 'mime' session. When placed at the back of the room and along two walls, another class can be accommodated during a lesson or audio-visual presentation. One class will sit on the tables, the other on the chairs or the floor. The tables can also be re-arranged to suit groupings of three, six, nine, twelve, fifteen, etc. They break with the tradition that a classroom and its arrangement shall be the same day in and day out, term after term, year after year.

This flexibility is increased if different areas of the classroom can be used for different activities. The inclusion of work-benches, for example, widens the range of approaches possible, as does a sink, a sand-tray, and a small corner where filmstrips or slides can be projected by individuals or groups. Alternatively, the back-projector could be housed here.

The preparation room

It has been seen that team teaching needs careful and possibly protracted planning. Periods could be written into the time-table for this purpose, although it is not often until a late stage in development that a headmaster realizes just how necessary this can be in terms of the initial preparation required. Special provision for such preparation is also extremely helpful as the general staffroom is clearly unsuitable for this purpose. One of the classrooms could be used for the various meeetings of the team, and this is satisfactory as long as they are held out of school hours and restricted to talk alone. However, such meetings are often held to consider the actual material to be used. A film has to be seen by a group of teachers, various uses of a filmstrip tried out, or a tape-recording edited. There has to be access to a wide range of equipment and materials unless the session is to be constantly interrupted whilst various items are brought from different areas of the school.

A 'preparation room' which can also serve as the nerve-centre of team-teaching operation is not quite the dispensible luxury it might at first sight appear. It can serve as a room for meetings and, if secure, as a storage depot for all the equipment used. Here also will be kept the records of slides, strips, and 'topics' referred to earlier (page 85), as well as record-cards relating to all the children taking part in the scheme. Visual-aids will be kept in cupboards whilst a summary of all meetings, an outline plan of current and proposed future developments, and a time-table of the scheme will be displayed on the walls. All copies of books currently being recommended for use will be available from this central point as well as a range of other aids and equipment.

The preparation room will be a working area, where materials can be arranged, and a meeting place for the team where decisions are taken. Such a 'nerve centre' is also valuable since teachers know exactly where to go to find the information required about staff, children, or equipment, without wasting valuable time searching all round the school.

Matching equipment to facilities

Needs created by materials and equipment largely speak for themselves. Suitable blackout equipment is obviously necessary in the rooms where projectors are to be used; tape-recorders have to be used where they will not disturb other classes, or adequate sound-proofing has to be installed. For convenience sake sockets throughout the rooms being used for team teaching should be of a uniform type. Spare plugs, fuses, and bulbs are also essential. Lack of a tiny 13-amp fuse, little bigger than a matchstick, can ruin a lead lesson that has taken several weeks to prepare. Some thought must also be given to the storage of this equipment. Security is one of the prior considerations, availability another. As has been seen,

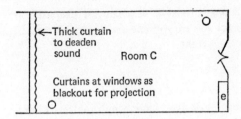

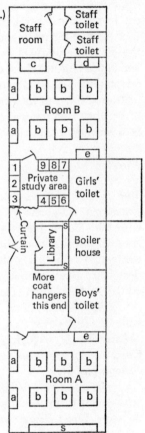

a = Working surfaces 1½ m. x 45 cm. (5 ft. x 18 in.)

b = Blockboard working surface on four desks

c = Bench for craftwork

d = Storage unit

e = Cupboard

s = Shelving

Room A

Art emphasis and materials

Private Study Area

Cut off from old cloakroom to provide nine study kiosks each lit separately

Library

Sufficient shelving well lit

Room B

Science and art surfaces and materials

Room C

No particular emphasis but could be used for projection

Annexe as I.D.E. centre © A. Aveling

both are taken care of by the provision of a central preparation room. Adequate storage space for equipment and materials within various classrooms is also important.

Self-help

Although several current school designs have been illustrated here, the emphasis thoughout the chapter has been upon changes that can be made to existing buildings to facilitate curricular innovation. One may be fortunate enough to obtain a grant for an extension to the existing buildings usually for a specific purpose, such as conversion to middle school or raising the school-leaving age, but most adaptations will be internal ones necessitated directly by the needs of team-work and integration.

The plan on page 101 shows how a fairly conventional annexe to a secondary school was converted for team-teaching purposes.

Further reading

The School in Contemporary Society by D. A. Goslin (Scott, Foresman, 1965) and *The Role of the School in a Changing Society*, edited by C. M. James and G. D. P. Phillips (Goldsmiths, 1965) are two publications which place this whole problem in a larger context. Children's opinions on educational architecture and design are given in no uncertain terms in *The School That I'd Like*, edited by E. Blishen (Penguin, 1969).

The Department of Education and Science Building Bulletins (HMSO) are a mine of information. Of special interest are *Schools in the U.S.A.* (1961), *Remodelling Old Schools* (1963), *Comprehensive Schools from Existing Buildings* (1968), and *Middle Schools* (1966).

Art and Craft in Education has a special feature on designing schools for team teaching in its August 1969 edition (pp. 2–4), as does the *Times Educational Supplement* of 28 November 1969.

9. *Assessing the work*

'Tricky little questions like . . . Prove
that u does not equal bf.'

Peter, 17

The assessment of a team-teaching scheme is an extremely
complex process. It is not sufficient merely to take a number of
schools using the technique and to compare them with several
organized along more conventional lines. For testing of this kind
to be scientifically valid, like has to be compared with like. Here the
aims of each school would probably differ and, if this were the
case, a different kind of team teaching would also emerge in each
one adopting such an approach.

Nor is it sufficient to take two schools where objectives are
entirely similar and compare the one being organized along team-
teaching lines with that run in the normal sort of way. This is getting
closer to what is required, but even so the staff will be different in
each school, the children come from differing backgrounds,
facilities will not be the same, nor will equipment, materials, time
alloted to the experiment, or the nature of the groupings. In
addition to this, the Hawthorne effect will have to be reckoned
with – children who know they are part of an experiment frequently
rise to the occasion and performance is higher than usual. Two
exactly corresponding schools, of course, will never be found, but
factors such as these will have to be taken into account before even
rough comparison is reached.

It may therefore be decided to carry out tests within a single
school, using several classes as 'control groupings'. These will
continue to be taught in the way they were before the introduction
of the technique. Similarly, different kinds of team approaches may
be tried out with the object of discovering which is the most
suitable for the particular school concerned. The patterns of team
teaching described in chapter four, where lead lessons are given
twice to two sets of three classes, opens up both these possibilities

to a school. Before anything like valid results can be achieved, though, as exact a balance as possible between the two groupings is necessary.

Obviously all this is primarily a task for specialists in the skills of educational testing and assessment. Those engaged in such studies need to be able to devote several years to a careful and detailed observation of each stage and of every factor. Work of this kind is now being carried out in several British universities (see page 17). Research in America is also in its early stages[1] but results obtained to date seem to indicate that, as far as factual knowledge and its interpretation are concerned, traditional methods score substantially when tested immediately after the completion of a unit of work. This knowledge, however, is not retained to anything like the extent that it is when 'team taught'. Tests carried out later show that – in the long run – team work pays handsome dividends. The material has significantly been 'made the pupil's own'.

Criteria for success

Teachers concerned with the day to day organization of team teaching will probably require more pragmatic and short-term methods of assessing the scheme as it develops. Their concern is likely to be focused on the effect such organization has upon individual standards of learning and attitude. They will want to know if the attitude of the pupil as expressed in his approach and achievement is really more positive under the technique. Will the less able suffer through weakness in the basic skills? Is retention of the material as extensive as it was under previous patterns of organization? Does co-operation of the kind claimed really take place within joint projects? Are the benefits for the staff involved really worth all the extra effort?

Before any attempt is made to examine the worth of a team-teaching scheme, its aims have to be isolated and clearly acknowledged. Similarly, before there can be an assessment of the pupil's work within such a scheme, agreement must be reached as to what the criteria for success are going to be. What are our scales of value? Do we prize retention of factual knowledge above or below a correct attitude towards the work and fellow pupils? Or is co-operative learning considered of the highest importance?

[1]   There is a good summary of this in *Team Teaching in Britain* by J. Freeman (Ward Lock, 1969), pp. 390–92.

Unless such a clarification of objectives is made and they are given some sort of order of priority, they could easily cancel one another out. If, for example, factual knowledge is regarded as important and tested by means of a monthly competitive examination, there is unlikely to be any co-operative pooling of knowledge or experience. Those who consistently languish at the bottom of a class, or group, are not really being encouraged to develop a positive attitude towards their work or their school. This may begin to show in a general deterioration in behaviour. Alternatively, if there is no test or examination and this is not replaced by some alternative stimulus, attitudes may appear to be good whilst very little of any consequence is being achieved.

When team teaching is introduced to stimulate effort within traditional divisions of departments and forms yet with no parallel organization to assist 'team learning', conventional methods of assessing progress may well serve. If the class is the unit and the syllabus composed of pieces of information to be learned in a certain order within a prescribed time, then the weekly test and the school examination will appear to be rational solutions. The end-product might even be GCE O or A level which, by their very nature, mean that each year some must pass and some must fail regardless of overall standards of attainment. In this case some will maintain that they are performing a kindness by preparing their pupils for such a classification. Others contend that, rather than gaining a true indication of individual merit in this way, we are merely conditioning some pupils to the concept of success and others to that of failure and, in so doing, are materially assisting the polarization of abilities. The CSE is currently in danger of being regarded in this way, too (see page 38), although the Mode 3 option remains open for those schools wishing to take it up.

Development of individual skills

Be this as it may, team teaching can be regarded in quite a different way – as a technique ruled by basic principles which, if carried through to their logical conclusions, cause a break with existing patterns of organization and traditional groupings of children. These new groupings of various size, either within the overall structure of the class or form, or existing without reference to it, together with the different kind of contribution called for from the staff, fresh treament of academic work, and new uses of materials, equipment, and facilities, all combine to make conventional forms of assessment unweildy and outdated.

If an initial stimulus to action is reinforced by a structuring in of individual skills and knowledge, set tests and examinations of these skills and this knowledge is difficult. Every child or each group within the year will have been exercising widely differing aptitudes, working at different aspects of the material. Not only this, but it can also endanger the concept of 'parity of esteem' outlined in chapter six. If certain skills – say writing or mathematics – are regarded as the more important contributions by members of the staff and understanding of the whole tested entirely through these channels, those children fortunate enough to be born with such aptitudes will be successful regardless of the total effort they have put into the work. This will appear both unrealistic and unfair to those whose skills lie in other fields. Nor can there be a really successful comparative examination of content, either oral, written, or by observation of work completed. How, for example, does one attempt to assess the relative values of a model of Stephenson's Rocket, a written account of the change brought about by the Industrial Revolution, and a recorded 'programme' on the 'Industries of Stockton on Tees'? In any case, the idea of examining work in this way brings in the element of competition which can destroy the concept of co-operation. But what alternative stimulus can be offered, and how can individual contribution and effort be assessed?

Stimulus is provided initially by the work itself and the incorporation of the talents possessed by each pupil. This is maintained in ways described earlier (page 76), but the individual will require further assurance that he is making progress and that his contribution is a worthwhile one. The teacher will need some basis upon which to ground that assurance and the school, quite rightly, will wish to have some estimate of what effort is being made by individual pupils and how they are progressing. Here surely is a case for comparing or contrasting the work done not with that of other pupils, but with each individual's own previous achievements.

Cumulative records

If this principle is introduced it means that a careful and cumulative account of the work done by the group as a whole must be kept, with a record of how this was sub-divided into 'topics' or areas, and the part played by each child in the work. These will have to be completed during and after each stage of the scheme and must, of course, be entirely confidential. Each school will have its own idea as to the aspects of the work it regards as being most important, but 'Attitude', 'Co-operation', and 'Development' will probably feature largely in all. The first will cover each pupil's response to lead lessons and readiness to help towards successful follow-up work. His basic contribution here will be assessed and the manner in which it is utilized noted. 'Co-operation' can be divided into a pupil's willingness to work alongside other children in a group and his attitude towards members of the staff with whom he comes into contact. 'Development' will initially assess his standing in the various basic skills. Some idea of where his strengths and weaknesses lie will also be plotted and tentative plans made as to how the areas of weakness can be approached through those of strength (see page 78).

There will therefore be a record of progress made under these various headings. Any remedial teaching to be done can be based upon the work in hand, and withdrawls of small sections of any class done as naturally as possible and related to this work.

Ideally, records of two kinds need to be kept. The first is a small card for each pupil, relating to the current topic tackled. It is completed by the teacher directing this part of the work and assesses the contribution made by the pupil as well as his 'rating' in the basic skills, various other aptitudes, and the traits considered important by the school. Each 'skill' or 'trait' is given a code letter, as can be seen in the illustration on page 108 and these are employed by all members of the team. a, for example, might represent Written Expression; b, Oral Proficiency; c, Mathematical Ability; etc. All team members also use the same form of marking – the 'five point scale' (A, B, C, D, E) or the 'ten point scale' (A—, B+, C, etc.), mark out of ten, or express the result as a percentage. Each teacher retains these record cards, which are extremely important in helping him to direct the work of each individual into the necessary channels, based on his 'needs'.

At the end of each term or each year, information from the record cards is transferred to record sheets (see page 109) which are kept in the central office or preparation room.

The very detailed information kept in this way can be of great value to other departments and also allows far more explicit reports to be sent home to the parents. This may even necessitate a new kind of report-form. Those currently in use, divided into small sections for the teacher's comments, positively invite such neutral comments as 'Satisfactory', 'Improving', or 'Could do better'. Something of the kind indicated on page 110 would serve the purpose of team teaching far more adequately.

Developmental patterns

Reference to certain questions a headmaster should ask himself at the very beginning of a team-teaching venture has already been made (page 33). In all probability the technique will fulfil the expectations put forward at the outset. If it does not, further examination of the reasons will be needed. Team teaching in practice will have to be carefully assessed alongside the objectives, both general and specific, set out at its inception. Changes in direction, policy, or organization may then seem clear. If either the headmaster is unwilling to make such changes or the staff

RECORD CARD

NAME_____ TEACHER _____

THEME_____

TOPIC_____DATES_____

GROUP_____

OTHERS IN GROUP_____

_____

BASIC CONTRIBUTION_____

COMMENT ON THIS_____

_____

RATING OF	RECOMMENDATIONS FOR FUTURE WORK
(a)	
(b)	
(c)	
(d)	
(e)	
(f)	
(g)	

YEAR I – RECORD SHEET

NAME_____

TEACHER(S)_____

GROUP(S)_____

WORK DONE_____

_____

_____

_____

_____

ASSESSMENT	RATING
ATTITUDE	
CO-OPERATION *a) with staff* *b) with other pupils*	
DEVELOPMENT	SKILLS *a)* *b)* *c)* *d)* *e)* *f)* *g)*

GENERAL COMMENTS

Signed _____

REPORT FORM

SUBJECT	WORK ACHIEVED	TEACHER'S COMMENTS
The Humanities	*a)* *b)* *c)* *d)* *e)* *f)* Progress made	
The Sciences	Work achieved *a)* *b)* *c)* *d)* *e)* *f)* Progress made	
The Arts	Work achieved	

*Signed*_____

(team co-ordinator)

of 'new wine' having come out of 'old bottles'. Its natural lines of development will have emerged and initiated the objectives and curricular reforms latent within it from the outset. What, though, are these 'lines of development'? What 'objectives' are endemic to team teaching?

Team teaching and curriculum development

These objectives are reflected in the three bases from which the team-teaching theory initially stems – the needs of the pupils; the contribution of the members of staff concerned in the scheme; and a variety of factors pertaining to each particular school or area (page 20).

Developmental team teaching strenuously works towards the subordination of all elements in a school which mitigate against a child's needs being met and to each member of staff making a full contribution towards the evolution and implementation of a suitable scheme of work. Thus, whilst 'school factors' such as existing materials, equipment, facilities, and curricular tradition have to be recognized at the outset, a further aim is the phasing out of such components as retrogressive elements, and their implementation as contributory factors in the overall planning of a team-teaching scheme.

Just how this takes place is a matter of conjecture, as different solutions will be arrived at by each school. The culminating phase of our cumulative diagram (see opposite), however, gives some indication as to the broad stages that might be involved.

Developmental sequence

It has been suggested that team teaching has certain incipient lines of development and that a realization of this can be helpful to those wishing to implement revisions of their school along more child-centred and less vicarious lines. The 'four rules' suggested for the introduction of any team-teaching scheme (page 112) must also be taken into account. The factors involved – time, patience, tact, and flexibility – are all important here. A knowledge of the general flow and direction that the technique is likely to take, and possession of these four essential virtues can give a blueprint by which team teaching can be introduced into a school.

There would seem to be nine clearly defined stages in this process which, taken together, form a logical sequence of curricular

concerned reluctant to work under them, the scheme may have to be brought to a close.

Team teaching, however, very often follows a developmental pattern of its own once it is set in motion. This pattern is dictated partly by the nature of the technique, partly by factors relating to the school, and partly by the personalities of the teachers involved. Unless hindered by lack of facilities or staff unease at changes that seem too rapid, the general movement appears to be from the formal to the informal, from a basically subject-centred approach to that of child-centred work. Speed and extent of this transition, of course, also depends very much on the age of the children and the area of the curriculum in which it is practised. But 'development' takes place in all successful team teaching ventures that are not harnessed to existing rigid forms of organization. Once this is realized and the general lines of development grasped, team teaching can become an acknowledged way of implementing curricular revision.

Further reading

For this chapter, the *Examination Bulletins* of the Department of Education and Science (HMSO) are important reading.

Few books are written on this topic, but *An Introduction to Educational Measurement* by D. Pidgeon and A. Yates (Routledge and Kegan Paul, 1969), *Developments in Educational Testing* edited by K. Ingenkamp (University of London Press, 1969), *Examinations – Pass or Failure* by W. B. Rust and H. P. F. Harris (Pitman, 1967), *Studies in Assessment* by J. F. Eggleston and J. F. Kerr, (English Universities Press, 1970) and D. McIntyre's article 'Assessment and Testing' in *Education for Democracy* (Penguin, 1970, pp. 166–75) are all available.

10. *Developmental team teaching*

'In the school I would like, the
relationship between teacher and
pupil would be changed. Instead of
the teacher telling the pupil, both
teacher and pupil would learn
together, creating warm relationships,
clear understanding and a zest for
knowledge.'

Judith, 13

By way of summary it can be said that two concepts of team teaching are currently in existence. It is either regarded as an administratively and economically convenient way of running a school, or as an educational technique in its own right having its own objectives and lines of development (see page 9).

An administrative framework

Looked at solely as an administrative framework, team teaching can be seen as enormously adaptive, being made to suit any level or area of curricular planning (pages 33–8). The ease with which it can be adapted has, in fact, tended to mitigate against its introduction on educational grounds. When fettered to inflexible forms of organization, team teaching may well be judged as inflexible and stereotyped itself. In fact whichever view is taken, the importance of careful and detailed planning is recognized. Four rules can be drawn up to assist in this, and in the actual introduction of the scheme into a school:

1. Team teaching cannot be introduced overnight. Time is required for it to take root (page 39).
2. Sophisticated forms of team teaching cannot be developed immediately (page 44).
3. Team teaching cannot be foisted on to a staff who do not want it (page 45).

4. There is no one method of organizing team teaching (page
Various patterns of overall planning can be used accor
to the age of the pupils, the area of the curriculum, and the na
of the material. Four such approaches were outlined in ch
four, being given the names 'Thematic', 'Concurrent', 'Sequen
and 'Concentric'. In presenting the material, the format of
lesson' and 'follow-up' will probably be used (see chapter
If team teaching is made to fit into existing academic struct
it may be confined to specific disciplines, the arrangement of
children for follow-up work being in accordance with the cur
pattern – streaming, setting, broad-banding, etc. If this is the
these follow-up periods will probably be confined to a fur
treatment of the overall theme along conventional lines, with
class teacher giving further lessons and setting class exercise
text-book reading. The facilities available may mitigate aga
any further development, or there may even be internal press
at work to contain further experimentation on the grounds
'dilution of academic standards' (see page 28).

'New wine – old bottles?'

However, from this point onwards new or revised uses of materi
equipment, and buildings might well seem necessary (chapt
seven and eight), and the children may be grouped in ways m
appropriate to these developments (chapter six). Relationsh
between them and the staff could become closer and more infor
whilst further changes in school organization now seem necessa
Mixed-ability groupings might seem the most relevant way
conducting follow-up work; some kind of interdisciplinary
integrated approach will almost certainly be called for if this do
not already exist; groups which cut across the traditional horizon
division into 'years' could be required; greater emphasis up
structuring the children's response into the planning of the sche
– making it far more 'open ended' in approach and 'child-centre
in design – will, perhaps, be felt necessary.

If this point is reached, it will have to be decided wheth
team teaching can remain confined within the existing structur
of the school, or whether changes in that structure are necessar
to free it? Should such revisions now be implemented, tea
teaching will have successfully bridged the gap between the tw
conflicting views mentioned earlier. This will, perhaps, be a cas

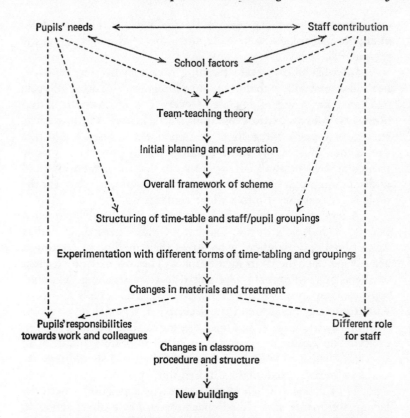

development. The staff of the school should first decide just how far they wish to proceed along these lines and which stage they have already reached. Purely local and personal factors may cause the telescoping of this whole process, the simultaneous development of two or more stages, or the omission of one or more of them. Before this is done, though, essential features of the stages concerned should be closely examined to ensure that they have either been satisfactorily covered or can, in the light of the current situation, be dispensed with. As much of the theory and practice contained within the sequence has been discussed in previous chapters, a brief sketch will suffice here.

Stage one

The initial stage lies in the appointment of new members of staff who may one day be called upon to form part of a team. The heads of department are of especial significance here. If the wrong kind of appointments have been made, the project will never get off the ground.

Interdisciplinary team teaching may well be contemplated, but it does not follow that in order to integrate with other subjects one must know something about every one of them. It is not necessary to know a little geography, a little history, a little science, etc., for successful integration. In pracitice it is often found that this comes most easily from teachers deeply interested in one particular field of study. It would seem that the greater love and understanding of a specific area of the curriculum, the stronger the basis is for merging it into a wider context.

A tendency for academic introversion is to be avoided when making such appointments. Candidates who regard their subject as an inviolate 'discipline', who stress their method of 'getting it across' and the benefits its inculcation will bestow may be excellent teachers, but are probably not suited to team teaching. The out-ward-looking approach is to be hoped for. This entails an extro-verted interest, based upon the security of personal involvement with one's own subject, and upon the curriculum considered as an entity. The candidate must not be blind to basic similarities in approach across wide areas of the curriculum and should indicate that he places the needs of the children above partisan introspection.

Most schools will find themselves in a position where the key appointments have already been made. More direct action on the introduction of team teaching will be felt necessary, which brings us to the next stage.

Stage two

This involves getting departments in the school working as teams within themselves. It implies no loss of status for the head of department, but rather a change of emphasis. He will now become far more of a co-ordinator of a group of individual men and women. Each will have his or her own skill and enthusiasm to contribute. It becomes the task of the head of department to mould these individuals into a successful team. This will mean regular meetings to review the current syllabus in the light of staff available, and to discuss organization within the department itself. It will mean adjusting the time-table so that exchanges can take place between teachers of different classes as often as needed, and provision made for two or more classes to come together where necessary. Methods of assessment will probably have to be revised. Familiarity with, and ease of handling a range of audio-visual aids will become necessary, as well as re-thinking along lines of lead-lesson and resourceful follow-up material.

Stage three

Greater cohesion within the department itself will probably be paralleled with closer contact with other departments in the school. This will come about through the more flexible time-tabling required which, in turn, necessitates co-operation on the part of other 'disciplines'. Stage three, then, would consist of building up this achievement and devising some more permanent means whereby departments meet together. Differing philosophies could be discussed but of greater importance each department will come to know exactly what work is going on throughout the rest of the school. There is a distinct possibility that, given such a structure – at present almost unknown in our schools – individual schemes of work may come to be internally modified and some common aims evolved.

Stage four

The next stage is a direct outcome of this sort of approach. Basic similarities in method and content, unknown when the department worked in isolation, will in all probability come to be seen in certain areas. This could very well lead to the occasional coming together of classes for joint lessons which cut across subject barriers. It could mean exchanges of teachers for isolated lessons or short programmes of work, and 'visiting' teachers coming in from other departments to supply their specialist knowledge or enthusiasm where it is appropriate.

Stage five

From here it is a quite big step to stage five – the official appearance of a scheme of integrated studies on the time-table. Quite probably pressure for this will by now be coming from the teachers themselves, but there is no reason why, at this point, suggestions and encouragement to work along such lines should not come from the headmaster himself.

At the outset such a project is almost bound to be tightly structured, formal in organization, and subject-centred in approach. The now familiar pattern of lead lesson and follow-up material is likely to emerge, with the work scrupulously apportioned between departments. The concept of the 'master teacher' may well emerge.

A fairly common example of this is the first year community study, where the geographical, historical, and religious aspects of the area are in turn illustrated. Other such schemes have already been described in passing (see pages 49 to 58).

To begin with each department is likely to want to keep follow-treatment of each lead lesson within its own hands. This leads to complexity of organization and, almost inevitably, to children being taken by different teachers in rotas. However, as the members of the team get to know one another better and become used to each other's methods of working; as the techniques and atmosphere of this kind of approach become more familiar, so a lot of the initial rigidity will be relaxed. It will be found that in a situaion such as this, where a group of teachers from different areas of the curriculum are actively at work in seeking a common denominator, the subjects concerned seem at first to 'blur at the edges' and then merge more fully into one another than at first anticipated. And so stage five almost imperceptibly merges into the next stage.

Stage six

The inflexible programme of set duration should now be on its way out as some are seen to merit fuller treatment, others to improve by compression. The programmes are also coming to be seen less as pure geography, history, religious education, or English, but rather to contain a mixture of all three in themselves. At this point it may well seem irrelevant for teachers to continue to teach only in their own disciplines. Indeed, what they teach may now appear to belong to no one 'discipline', and a new title sought – 'the humanities', or 'humanity', for example.

Stage seven

It is when this point has been reached that stage seven has arrived. A joint team can now begin discussions as to the individual potentials and enthusiasms of it members, rather as the individual departments did in stage two. Again as in stage two, it is to be hoped that a forward-looking syllabus will emerge. By now it may be time for a general co-ordinator to be appointed should there be an obvious and indisputable choice from among the team.

Stage eight

Having come this far, another element usually enters the scheme. Stage eight is generally characterized by the emergence of children's reactions as a factor in planning and modification. The complete scheme, and each section of it, will come to be by the way it meets the needs of those for whom it is intended (see page 19). Not infrequently the children will determine, by their obvious enthusiasm or lack of it, the lines along which development should take place. It would be a strangely inflexible teacher who did not respond to such direction.

Stage nine

The final stage will now have been reached. Lead lessons as they have hitherto been known are largely a thing of the past. The characteristics of team teaching at this stage are – the choice of a wide and very general theme by the team – say, 'Population', 'The Middle East', 'Industrialization', or 'The Middle Ages'. There will be an initial stimulus, in which the combined resources of a now fully-integrated team are brought to bear to give an imaginative, colourful, and vivid treatment of the topic. The children will re-act to this in a multitude of ways. Groups of children, probably of different sizes, will then be formed, or merge naturally, and several groups be assigned to a member of the team according to his or her special interests. Groups will then work with batches of material – work-sheets, work-cards, slide-viewers, reference books, pictures, pre-recorded tapes, modelling equipment – provided beforehand by the team. From these groups will come material which can be placed together and around which centre a variety of 'comings together' of larger groups. These meetings act as secondary stimulation. Each child can see exactly how his work fits into that of the group and, in turn, how his group's work relates to that of the year.

The children now appear to be having a direct hand in the nature, extent, and pace of the work, The original 'team' of teachers, presenting what they believed it would be beneficial for the children to know, has been superseded by a variety of other teams, as indicated in chapter six (see pages 76 to 82).

Transformation of existing structures

Great stress has been laid throughout this book on the developmental aspects of team teaching.

One does not wish for change simply for its own sake, but I personally would have deep suspicions about any scheme which ceased to evolve and had become static. The assumption would be that one had 'arrived'; that the 'needs' of this year's children were identical with the 'needs' of last year's; that changes in staff brought no fresh energies, expertise, skills, or enthusiasms into play; that team teaching to date had had little or no effect upon the administration of the school, the organization of the classroom, or the facilities available.

'Pupils' needs'; 'staff contribution'; and 'school factors' are the three theoretical bases of team teaching. Attention to them is bound to bring change in its wake; change which, in turn, will engender still further curricular revision. It is my own belief that, by the time the final stage in the above outline has been reached, these three original factors will have been transformed as illustrated in the diagram on page 115. Team teaching may well then appear totally different from our original concept of it, presenting a new theoretical basis for future development.

It could be said that transformation of existing structures is endemic to the whole process of team teaching and that it has taken a period of almost unprecedented change within our schools to bring it into existence. Surely, though, transformation or change is a characteristic feature of education itself. This being the case, it may be that team teaching as we now know it represents the schooling of the future in embryo.

Author's footnote

Comments on any points raised in this book would be most welcome. I can be reached through the publishers and am especially interested in hearing about team-teaching schemes in progress, new uses of equipment or materials, and new patterns of organization.

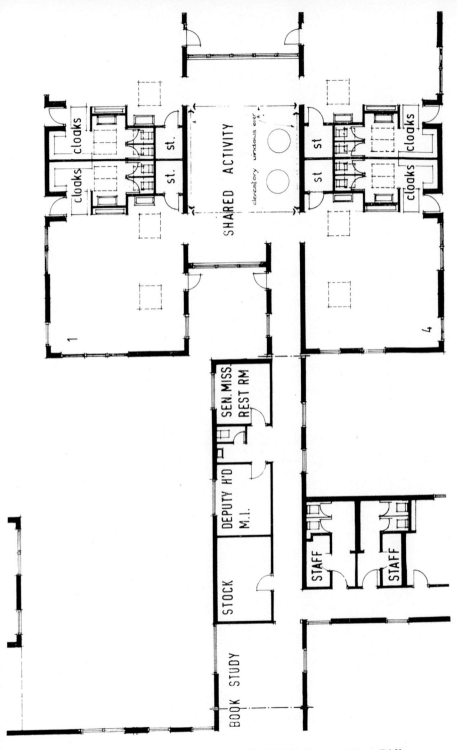

An extract from the plans for Hatfield Middle School, West Riding

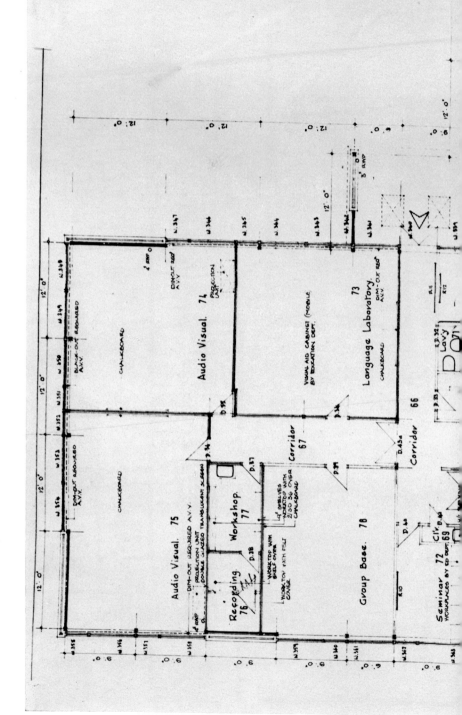

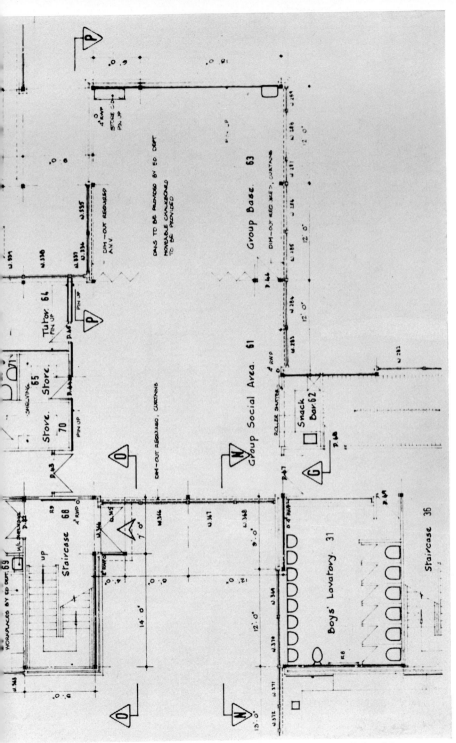

An extract from the plans for Merrywood Comprehensive School for Boys, Bristol

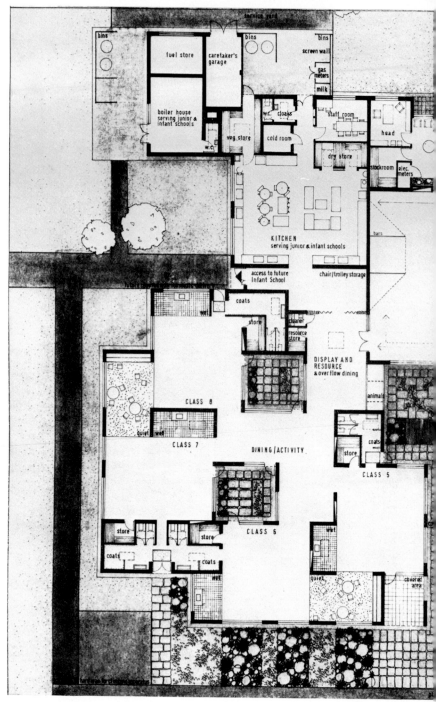

The architect's plans for
Junior Middle

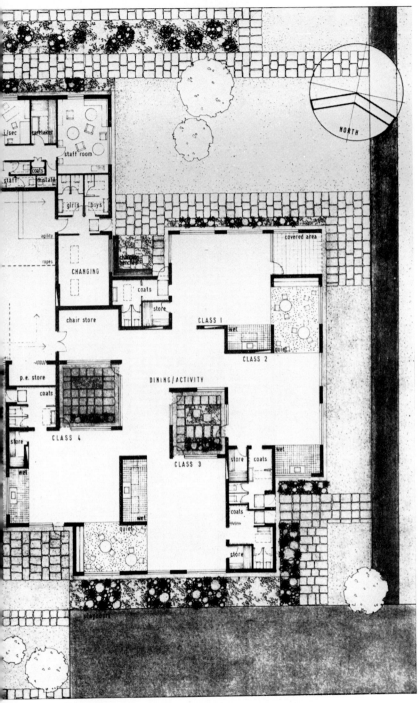

...herby Deighton Gates
..., West Riding

An extract from the plans for the John Smeaton
Comprehensive School, Leeds

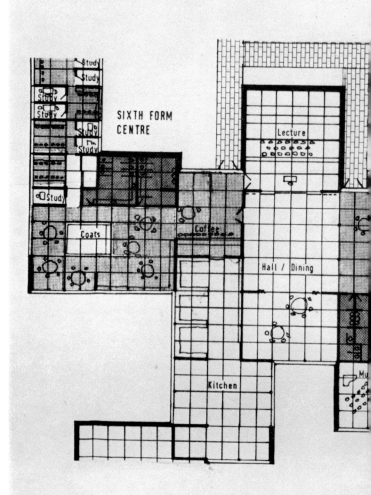

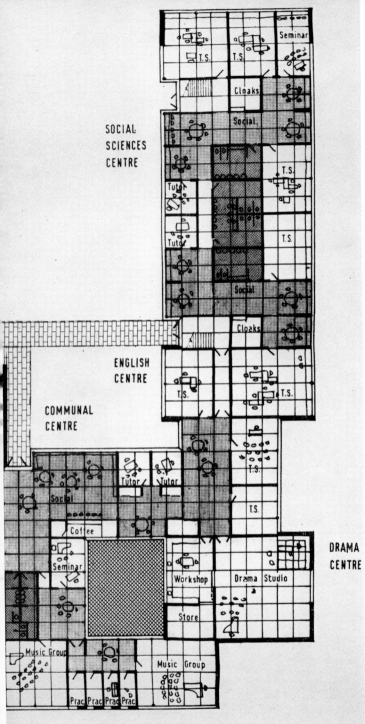

SOCIAL
SCIENCES
CENTRE

Seminar

T.S.

T.S.

Cloaks

Social

T.S.

Tutor

T.S.

Tutor

T.S.

Social

Cloaks

ENGLISH
CENTRE

COMMUNAL
CENTRE

T.S.

T.S.

T.S.

Tutor

Tutor

T.S.

Social

T.S.

Coffee

Seminar

DRAMA
CENTRE

Workshop

Drama Studio

Store

Music Group

Music Group

Prac Prac Prac Prac

MUSIC CENTRE

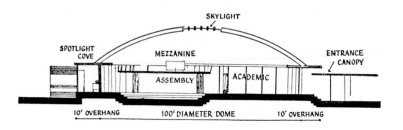

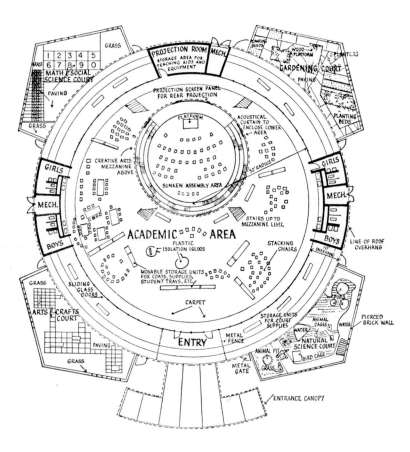

Domed elementary school adjacent to Queens College, New York City. Designed by Caudill, Rowlett and Scott, Architects-Planners-Engineers of Houston, Oklahoma City and Stamford, Connecticut

KING ALFRED'S COLLEGE

LIBRARY

Index

ability, 70, 74, 76, 79
adviser, 44
aesthetics, 13, 36
aides, non professional, 15
aids, audiovisual, 13, 15, 20, 90–3,
   117
   duplicated, sheets, 62, 63, 80
   teaching, 60, 83–4
   visual, 43, 60, 90–1, 100
aims of team teaching, 33, 104–5,
   111
Anderson, R., 16
aptitude, 74, 76
assessment, of pupil, 20, 36
   of team teaching, 103–11
attitude, *see* children
Aveling, A., 101

Barnes, M. W., 14
bay, 97
blackboard, 42, 61, 96, 97
black-out, 42, 97, 100
Bolan, D. W., 17
booklets, 85, 87
brains trust, 37, 43
buildings, 19, 41–2

cameras, 8 mm, 91
   35 mm, 90
careers guidance, 38
carrels, 96

cataloguing, 90
Certificate of Secondary
   Education, (CSE), 38, 105
chairs, 41–2
children, attitude of, 104
   co-operation of, 107
   development of, 20
   interests of, 74
   needs of, 11, 12, 19, 20, 28, 34,
      40–1, 67, 96–8, 120
   participation of, 61–2
   reactions of, 119
   response of, 107
   social needs of, 20, 41
   universal needs of, 41
Clarke, W. F., 47
classes, 10, 20, 26–7
classroom, 20, 41
   exhibitions, 79, 80
   libraries, 85
class teaching, 80
clip boards, 88
closed-circuit television, 92–3
competition, 74
   in examinations, 105
concentric pattern, the, 57–8
conferences, 30, 45
co-operation, 30, 74, 104
co-ordinator, general, 19, 116, 119
counsellor, 14
courses, 18, 44

creativity, 36, 54
cumulative sequence, the, 56–7
curriculum, 28, 29, 31, 38, 95
  see also headmaster
  traditional, 10–13
curriculum development centre,
  45

department, academic, 10, 29
  heads of, 10, 19, 23, 36, 40,
    65–6, 115–16, 117
  organization of, 23–6, 116, 117
  subject, 23, 27, 52, 65
discovery techniques, 83
drama, 42, 68, 78

educational games, 83
environment, 34, 38
epidiascope, 43
equipment, 18, 19, 20, 42–4,
  88–93
  audiovisual, 24
examinations, 35–7
  competitive, 105
  external, 37
exercise books, 87
exhibition, 60, 63, 64
  classroom, 79, 80
extension leads, 90, 97

facilities, school, 19
faculties, 35
files, loose-leaf, 87–8
filmstrips, 23, 24, 43, 88–91, 100
Fitton, N., 30
flexibility, 14, 34, 35, 66, 87, 116
flexible school, 27, 95–102
flexible time-table, 117
folders, 85
  see also files
follow-up work, 19, 25, 26, 50,
  60, 67–9, 73, 76, 87, 97, 118
forms, *see* classes
Freeman, J., 17, 21, 104
furniture, 97, 99

General Certificate of Education
  (GCE), 35, 38, 105
general studies, 37
gifted child, 73, 79–80

group, American classification, 14
  control group, 103
  corporate needs, 41
  leader, 26
  matching to task, 20
  mixed-ability, 17, 113
  size/composition, 12, 13, 14, 24,
    36, 41, 66, 67, 68, 70–82,
    113, 119
  work, 16, 17, 26

hall, 36, 41, 96
Hawthorne effect, 103
headmaster, 18, 33, 39, 44, 45,
  99, 111, 117
  position of, 10, 11, 12
humanities, 13, 36, 118
  see also project

illustrations, home-made, 91
individual, contribution, 62,
  76–9
  needs of, 40–1, 96, 114
  skills, 105–11
  study, 14, 38
information, recording of, 54
integrated studies, 27–9, 36, 95,
  117
integrated day, 57
interdiscipliary team-teaching,
  36, 116
internships, 15
interview, 91
item banks, 83, 87, 92

joint lesson, 117

King, R., 17

late developer, 72
learning, team, 105
  see also project
leaver, early, 37–8
lesson, joint, 117
lesson, lead, 19, 24–5, 26, 34, 36,
  41, 42, 50, 60–4, 67, 68, 73,
  81, 87, 96, 103, 118, 119
  teachers and, 24, 61, 63
  time, 62
  varieties of, 62–4

levels of aspiration, 72, 74, 79–80
library, 80, 85, 97
  class, 85
  sound, 92
Lloyd Trump, J., 15
locality, *see* neighbourhood
Lovell, K., 16

master teacher, 118
materials, 18, 19, 87–8
  audiovisual, 20, 23
  follow-up, 26
  pre-recorded, 90
  taped, 92
meetings, 19, 39–40, 50, 51, 68,
    100, 117
  see also conferences
methods, project, 16
  teaching, 28, 30
Middle School, 34
mime, 68, 78, 99
minority studies, *see* general
    studies
mixed-ability teaching, 39, 72–3,
    75–8, 95
Mode Three, *see* CSE
motivation, 14

National Association of Secondary
    School Principals, 14
National Education Association,
    14
neighbourhood, 16, 26, 38, 86, 88,
    118
Newsom children, 74
note-taking, 61–2
Nuffield Foundation, 17, 83
Nuffield Science, 95

objectives, educational, 20–1
Olds, H. F., 14
organization, academic, 70–2
  new patterns, 13
  school, 21
orienteering, 83

participation, *see* children
philosophy, of team teaching, 27

photography, 43, 90
physical education, 10
planning, 14, 39–44, 45, 78, 112–13
  periods, 99
plans, *between* 120 and 121
potential, innate, 20, 40, 41, 74
practical subjects, 36
preparation, 19, 39, 86–7
  room, 99–100, 107
pre-recording, 90–1, 92, 119
presentation, 'key', 18
press conference, 64
programme, 44, 50, 52, 55, 57,
    60, 93, 118
programmed learning, 83, 92–3
programming, 60–9
Project, Resources for Learning, 17
  Humanities Curriculum, 17
projector, back, 60, 99
  8 mm, 91
  overhead, 43, 62, 91
  strip, 90
psychology, faculty, 28
pupils, *see* children

questionnaire, 62, 85
questions, 61

record, cards, 100, 107, 108
  sheets, 107
records, cumulative, 106–11
  of text-books, 85
Redfearn, Mrs C., 87, 90
remedial teaching, 107
report form, 111
resource, area, 97
  packs, 83, 85
Richardson, E., 17
Rollings, A. B., 30
rooms, for follow-up work, 97–8
  preparation, 99–100
Rudd, W. G. A., 17

sample studies, 57
sand tray, 99
scale, five and ten point, 107

school, design, 96–102
  facilities, 19–20
  leaver, 36–8, 57
  leaving-age, 16
  organization, 10–13, 21, 23–5,
    26, 34–5, 70–2, 95, 113–14
  upper secondary, 26, 34–6
schools,
  Brockington High,
    Leicestershire, 87, 90
  Death Valley High, 97, 98
  Hatfield Middle, 97, plans
    section
  John Smeaton
    Comprehensive, Leeds, 98,
    plans section
  Merrywood Comprehensive,
    Bristol, 97, plans section
  St. Helier Boys, Jersey, 47
  Wetherby Deighton Gates, 96,
    plans section
Schools Council, 16, 17, 83
  General Studies Project, 17
  Working Papers, 38
Schools Museum Service, 64
Sciences, The, 13, 43
setting, 71
Shaplin, J. T., 14
simulation exercises, 14
sixth form, 35
  see also team teaching
skills, 27, 104, 106
  basic, 93, 104
  individual, 105–11
  subject, 29
slides, *see* films
slow learners, 15, 72, 74, 75,
  79–80
sockets, 97, 100
sound proofing, 100
speakers, visiting, 43, 64, 87
specialist, 24, 27
specialization, 71
staff, appointments, 115
  co-operation, 30–1
  deployment, 25–6
staffroom, 30
Stenhouse, L., 17
stimulation, secondary, 80–2, 119

stimulus, 19, 106, 119
streaming, 70, 73, 74
  broad band, 71
  and gifted child, 80
  of staff, 72
students, 15
study-kit, 87
subject, barriers, 31
  departments, 23, 27, 52–3, 65
  disciplines, 12, 27–8, 34, 39, 116
  divisions, 27, 39
  integration, 16, 52–4
syllabus, 12, 13, 23, 26, 27, 40,
  93, 116, 119

tape recorder, 43, 90, 92, 97, 100
Taylor, L. C., 17
teachers, 12, 13, 15, 21
  as counsellor, 14
  enthusiasm, 25
  exchange of, 55, 117
  general subject, 10
  interchange, 41
  isolation, 30–1
  and lead lesson, 24, 61, 63
  master, 118
  role in team teaching, 12–13, 15,
    19, 40, 78–9, 116
  teams of, 55, 57
  time of, 26
  traditional role, 23–7, 30–1,
    75–6
teachers' centres, 17, 83, 87
teaching, kits, 83, 89
  machines, 92–3
team learning, 105
team-work, 19, 30, 50, 55, 82,
  119–20
team teaching, academic
    organization, 49–53
  assessment, of, 103–11
  characteristic features, 25
  and closed-circuit television,
    92–3
  definition, 18–20
  developmental, 21, 44, 111–20
  developments in England, 16–18
  diagrammatic representation, 69
  and early leaver, 37–8

economic factors, 23–6
and examination classes, 36–7
in lower school, 33–4
in upper school, 34–8
integrated, studies, 27–30, 36, 39
mixed-ability grouping, 73–5, 76–82, 113
organization of, 18, 27, 60–9, 73
origins, American, 14–16
origins, English, 16–18
planning/preparation, 33
sixth form, 37
theoretical basis, 9–13, 20, 120
television, 42
tests, educational, 104
objective, 40
text-books, 84–6
thematic approach, 49–56
themes, 'Composition of Our World', 51–2
'Communities', 58
'The Elements', 50
'Impressionistic Art/Music', 55
'Industrialization', 119
'Man's Conquest of His World', 53–4
'Me', 57–8
'Middle Ages', 76, 119
'Middle East', 119

'Population', 119
'This Motorbike', 58
time-table, 12, 13, 18, 20, 42, 100, 116, 117
blocking, 27, 62
double periods, 68
planning periods, 99
topic, 36, 50, 53–4, 85, 107, 119
'Coal', 60
concurrent, 55–6
'Earth', 53–4
'Mediaeval Village', 77
'Voyages of Discovery', 60
training, in-service, 18, 44
transition, primary to secondary school, 29, 34
tutorials, 36, 41

University of York, 17
unstreaming, approaches to, 75
and gifted child, 80
and slow learner, 80

validity, scientific, 103
values, moral, 20
visits, outside, 60, 63–4

work-cards/sheets, 63, 80, 85–7, 119
working parties, 40
workshops, 83, 87